CAUGHT IN THE current

CAUGHT IN THE current

Searching for Simplicity in the Technological Age

Jay Bookman

St. Martin's Press ❧ New York

www.stmartins.com

Library of Congress Cataloging-in-Publication Data

Bookman, Jay.
    Caught in the current : searching for simplicity in the technological age / Jay Bookman.—
1st ed.
        p. cm.
    ISBN 0-312-30925-2
    EAN 978-0312-30925-1
    1. Technology and civilization.   I. Title.

T15.B64 2004
303.48'3—dc22

2003070103

10 9 8 7 6 5 4 3 2

To Julie, who saw it before I could

caveat lector

This is, among many other things, a story about an annual white-water rafting trip among five friends. Such a tale may raise the question of whether it is fact or fiction.

I choose to answer this way:

If such a trip actually took place, if a river such as the Deschutes really existed, you might imagine some of the author's companions insisting that he change their names, and in some cases use composite characters. They might even insist that the author deny the existence of the Deschutes, in an attempt to protect the river that they love.

So if you happen to see a map of Oregon showing the Deschutes River, please pay it no heed. The place does not exist.

Really.

acknowledgments

This book grew out of research into the social impact of technology funded by the Eugene Pulliam Fellowship, sponsored by the Society of Professional Journalists. As that research took manuscript form, Richard Dobkin, Steve Visser, Susan Wells, and Teresa Weaver offered valuable guidance and encouragement. I'd also like to thank Larry Swindell, who graciously allowed use of his Alfred Manuel Pesano story; and Cynthia Tucker and *The Atlanta Journal-Constitution* for their patience.

Finally, I have to acknowledge Alan Bookman, Stewart Day, Larry Messick, Steve Olson, Ted Test, and Jay F. Wallace for their grudging willingness to let me tell our stories.

CAUGHT IN THE current

day one

Shackles come in many forms and guises.

A few years ago, I had the chance to pick up and hold a set of cast-iron shackles made some two hundred years ago, probably by a slave blacksmith forced to hammer out the tools of his own confinement. The iron felt brutishly heavy in my hand, the soft metal ringing a dirge of the Georgia plantation where they had been forged and used. I couldn't help but think about all the people, maybe hundreds of them, who had felt the weight of those shackles around their wrists and ankles.

The human mind can be shackled too, of course, not by iron but by fears and misconceptions that hobble the imagination just as surely as those shackles hobbled the legs of plantation slaves. Mental shackles make it impossible to imagine a world other than this one—they confine their victims' minds to a pitifully small space in which to roam.

Then there are the shackles devised to confine the human spirit, the kind that we human beings impose on each other. In New York Harbor, Lady Liberty stands with torch aloft as a symbol of freedom from such oppression. At her feet, a set of shackles lays empty.

To my mind, though, the most dispiriting shackles are those we clamp on ourselves. We seldom think of them as shackles—that's part of their menace. They ingratiate themselves into our lives like little Iagos, posing as dutiful servants while subtly undermining what we hold most precious.

Consider my watch and cell phone, now sitting side by side next to my employee ID badge back in Atlanta. They are merely tools, just inanimate sources of information that help get me through my day. But they must be something more as well. Because yesterday morning, when I placed my watch and cell phone in a heap on the top of my dresser and headed for the airport, I felt a twinge of guilty pleasure, as if I were a dog quietly slipping its leash.

Just now, out of habit, I glanced down at my wrist to check the time and instead saw the pale swath of flesh where the watch usually sits.

And I smiled. I've slipped the shackles . . . for the next week or so anyway.

Every August for the past ten years, four friends and I have taken a rafting trip down the Deschutes River canyon in central Oregon. Sometimes we invite one or two others along as well, but at a minimum it's always been the five of us. Over the years, none of the core group has missed a trip.

By now it has become part of my inner rhythm: Just as late October means Halloween and late December means Christmas, August means the Deschutes. The river is a beautiful place: class 3 and 4 white-water rapids, great fishing, a stark desert landscape, and black, star-filled nights so peaceful that the world makes sense of itself again. Things simplify out on the river.

And when it's over, when September rolls around and vacations end and life turns serious again, I bring a little bit of that peace home with me. It's in my head, accessible in daydreams whenever I need to visit.

Of course, getting ready for a trip like this takes a lot of work. I fly in from Atlanta, my brother arrives from Austin, and a third member of our crew, Stewart, comes in from Nashville. The twenty-four hours before we hit the river are always a blur of airport shuttle runs and errands and shopping trips, of checking equipment, packing lists, and menus.

Inevitably, though, a magical moment comes when all the planning and packing is finished and the checks have been written, when all the forms have been filled out and there are no more fishing licenses, boating permits, or raft rental agreements to sign.

All that's left is to go.

This is that moment. Just a few minutes ago, in the grocery store parking lot, I even pulled my wallet out of my back pocket and stowed it away in the bottom of an equipment bag. Where I'm going, they won't be taking American Express.

Or Visa either.

The afternoon is truly beautiful, a late-summer day of blue skies, bright sunshine, and cool mountain air. My friend Richard is behind the wheel of his apple red Yukon, taking us up U.S. 26, along the southern flank of Mount Hood in north-central Oregon. I'm in the passenger seat beside him, with our three other crew members crammed into the backseat.

The mountainside around us is humming, busy with people coming and going from the forest campgrounds and trails accessible from the highway. Through the window, it looks as though someone had jammed a stick into a hive of angry SUVs. They're everywhere you look—Land Rovers, Cherokees, Broncos, Troopers.

They're lining up at intersections, zipping down the highway, pulling in or out of fast-food joints, everybody heading somewhere in a hurry. And every vehicle is crammed to the roof with camping gear and sleeping bags. Some, like our own, are towing trailers to carry the overflow.

One hundred fifty years ago, this was the route of the old Barlow

Road, one of the roughest portions of the Oregon Trail. Thousands of settlers passed through here in the 1840s, headed west in covered wagons to Oregon City, and from there into the rich Willamette Valley. Things have changed a lot since then—the road's a lot better, for one thing. But the landscape is still rugged, the views magnificent. Even now it's easy to imagine the struggle it must have been to haul those wagons up and down these steep mountainsides. In fact, if you hike down one of the trailheads we just passed, you can still find wagon ruts carved into the soil by the string of Conestogas traveling westward.

Today, though, we're headed east, up through little mountain towns with poetic names such as Rhododendron, Zigzag, and Government Camp. The Deschutes canyon is still about sixty miles away, but with all the chores finally behind us, the anticipation is beginning to build.

"Hey J-Book," someone says from the backseat. "You better look at your brother."

I twist around in my seat to see Alan, his tackle box on his lap, busily at work on his fishing reel.

"Whatcha doing back there, Alan?" I ask.

"Oh . . . nuttin'," he says, keeping his head bent over his work. I can't see his face, but I just know he's grinning.

I know what Alan's doing. Shoot, we all know what he's doing. He intends to be ready the moment the Yukon comes to a halt at the campsite. He wants to open the door, march toward the river with his fishing rod, and be the first to toss a lure into the current.

"You fish slut," I say.

Alan still doesn't lift his head from his work, but I know his smile is even bigger now. The other two guys in the back, Stewie and Marv, start rummaging around as well, digging out their own fishing gear. The fever has spread. It's a contagion.

Richard reaches up to adjust his rearview mirror, slanting it down so he can peer directly into the backseat.

"Hey! Buy a new reel, A-Book?" Richard asks, staring into the mirror, snapping his eyes back to the road, then peering into the mirror once more. "What is that? Looks like a Quantum 6000."

That brings Alan's head up. He stares into the mirror, into the reflection of Richard's eyes, then shakes his head.

"You can see that? From up there?"

"Sure. I looked at one of those in the store last week. I looked at the 4000 too, but it doesn't have that automatic flip-bail, right? You made a good choice. A little more money, but damn well worth it in my opinion."

The rest of us crack up. Richard loves equipment, and he takes a lot of pride in it. "Richard Gear," we call him. If there's a newfangled piece of camping equipment on the market—a pop-up tent one year, a three-in-one flashlight another year—Richard will show up with it.

I have to admit, though, that over the years he has bailed out every one of us when we've forgotten, lost, or broken a piece of equipment. His assistance doesn't come for free, though. Oh no. He will make you pay for it.

"Oh, did Jay Bookman forget to bring his hook file?" he'll say as I stand like a supplicant in front of him. "Why, Jay, I don't know that I have an extra one I could lend you. I've got one for myself, of course. Wouldn't go fishing without it. You need a file to sharpen your hooks, and as I'm sure you know, sharp hooks catch more fish. But I'll have to look to see if I've got another one with me."

And all the while he damn well knows, like I damn well know, that he brings at least two of everything on the trip.

But the river has a way of getting you back. Last year we had just shoved off from the launch site and were floating downstream, thrilled that the trip was finally under way, when Richard realized that his fishing vest—equipped like Noah's ark with two of everything—had somehow been left behind inside the Yukon.

And as we looked toward shore, all we could do was watch helplessly as a shuttle driver pulled the red Yukon and its now-empty trailer out of the boat-launch area and onto the highway, headed north to our designated take-out spot, where it would be waiting for us when we finished the trip.

We were all stunned, but no one more than Richard. At first he was angry, certain that it had been somebody else's mistake. But he couldn't come up with a plausible scenario for how somebody else could have been responsible. It was, after all, his vest. And on the river each man is ultimately responsible for his own equipment.

So he sank into a sullen pout.

He wasn't going to fish this trip, he announced. Nobody stupid enough to forget his entire fishing vest should be allowed to fish the Deschutes anyway. He would just row his raft and watch the rest of us fish. Would serve him right.

Now, this wasn't really a serious turn of affairs. Between us, we had more than enough extra gear to get Richard set up again.

But none of us said a thing. If Richard wanted help, he was going to have to ask, which a couple of hours later he finally did. His raftmate, Stewie, gave him enough lures, swivels, and weights to get him through the first day of fishing. And that night at camp we all donated enough equipment to outfit him completely. I even had an extra vest to give him.

"When we get there, remind me to show you *my* new reel," Richard says to Alan, calmly tapping the rearview mirror twice on the top, then a touch on the bottom to return it to its previous position. "It'll put that little 6000 of yours to shame."

The rest of us burst out laughing again.

I turn to look out the window, at the scenery passing us by. The Pacific Northwest is famous for lush, deep green rain forests, towering

Douglas firs, and clear mountain streams, and for the moment that's exactly what surrounds us. The trees on either side of the highway rise 150 feet straight into the sky, the branches creating a canopy so tight that it blocks the sun from the dark forest floor. Everything is so green and damp it almost hurts to look.

Off to our left, rising high above the trees, you can see snow-capped Mount Hood, reaching an elevation of more than eleven thousand feet. It's one of a range of volcanic mountains, called the Cascades, that runs up and down the Pacific Coast, extending north into Canada and south into California.

The most famous peak in the range is Mount St. Helens, which made world headlines when it erupted in 1980. Like St. Helens, Hood is an active volcano—in fact, vulcanologists were surprised that St. Helens, not Hood, became the first to erupt in the modern era.

Looking at all this, it's hard to believe that in another twenty minutes we'll be traveling through harsh desert, with nothing green in sight. We're at the eastern boundary of the rain forest; beyond it lies the water-starved Great Basin.

The dividing line between the two ecosystems is the Cascades. As storms roll eastward off the Pacific, heavy with moisture, they ram up against these mountains and begin to dump their load of rain, turning this area into a temperate rain forest, lush and green. The Cascades force the storms to climb higher and higher, wringing the moisture out of them as they rise. By the time the clouds are high enough to pass over Mount Hood and its sisters, they've been wrung dry, mere wisps of their former selves.

As a result, the western flank of these mountains gets over a hundred inches of rain a year. Just a little farther up the road, in the high desert, precipitation drops to about ten or twelve inches a year.

You can already see hints that a climate change is coming. With each mile we travel, the Douglas fir trees have gotten a little more sparse, the vegetation a little less lavish. The mix of trees is beginning to change as well. Biologists call places like this an ecotone, a zone between one type of ecosystem and another. It's an edge, where one thing teeters on the verge of becoming another.

And there it is. I never get over how suddenly it happens. We pop over the crest of a ridge and suddenly the desert spreads out before us. A few miles back you might be able to peer a hundred feet into the green forest dimness. Now you can gaze out over a hundred miles of blue sky and bright sun-washed desert, with a series of high, snowcapped peaks—Mount Jefferson, the Three Sisters, Three-Fingered Jack—lining the western horizon, marching south toward California.

It takes a moment for your eyes, and your brain, to adjust to the change in scale out here. There's something feminine and enveloping about the deep forest, but the openness of the desert calms in a different way. It's an evolutionary thing, probably, a sense of safety in being able to see trouble coming—or game approaching—from miles away. It's the instinct that draws people to build their homes on hilltops and mountains. The open vista pulls the stress right out of you.

Once out onto the open desert, Richard flips on the radar detector mounted on his dashboard, and the car seems to pick up speed in response.

Our destination for the night is a spot called Trout Creek, a campground run by the federal Bureau of Land Management and one of the few places on the lower Deschutes accessible to the public by vehicle. Even then you have to know it's there, because I've never seen Trout Creek on any road map. It's down at the bottom of the Deschutes canyon, at the end of a very bumpy, dusty, poorly marked road.

We're all eager to get to the river, to see it and smell it and feel the desert heat on our backs again. By now the place has become as familiar to us as our own living rooms.

In fact, I've sometimes caught myself giving in to the notion that places such as the Deschutes are the "real world," where we human beings would be living if we hadn't lost our senses some time back. It's certainly the antithesis of the "made world" of computers and beepers and business lunches.

But in truth, the real world is the place we're leaving behind right now, the place where we make our living, raise our children, live and die and prosper and fail. The river and other natural areas are little more than human playgrounds now, places where we pick up a different set of toys, and a different set of challenges, and run off and have fun.

Back in that real world, I work as a journalist. Years ago, when I started out in newspapers, my goal had been to become a foreign correspondent, because at the time that's where the action was, the place where you could see the world being remade. But at some point back in the early nineties, I began to realize that the arena of change had itself changed, that the catalyst for the stunning revolution taking place around me was now science and technology. I began to gravitate toward that area, and ever since then, thanks to my job, I've had a ringside seat at some of the most remarkable transformations in human history.

I've watched in awe as a lab technician nonchalantly punctured the wall of a human egg cell and with a gentle exhale blew a human sperm inside—literally giving the egg the breath of life. I've lain in a machine—my head surrounded by superconducting electromagnets—while a researcher watched how my brain tissue responded to visual and written stimuli. And I've stood in a room full of the industry's top software people, all of them arrogantly aware of their own brilliance and some of them millionaires many times over, only to see them melt into a hushed awe when "Bill"—Bill Gates—entered the room.

In many ways, though, the most interesting part of the experience has been doing what everyone else has been doing, just trying to stay functional in the new world that technology is creating. In my job I've seen the tools as they start to emerge from the laboratory, and then, like everyone else, I've watched them take on a life of their own once they're introduced, affecting how we live in ways that no one had anticipated. Keeping current with technology has become a critical part—often *the* critical part—of almost every profession, and a challenge in daily life as well.

For many science journalists, the appeal of the job lies in the machines themselves, in the often marvelous and creative ways that scientists and engineers rearrange the world around them. While I share that interest, I'm even more intrigued by the way we humans interact with our creations and inventions. It's not the tools, but the way we use them, that fascinates me.

For example, I'm puzzled by the way we behave as passive recipients of technological change. Human beings, who by nature accept almost nothing as unalterable, who as a species have traveled to the moon and have learned to manipulate matter at its most fundamental levels, still treat their own technology as a force they dare not challenge, confront, or even analyze too closely. That perplexes me.

One common explanation is the so-called technological imperative, the fatalistic notion that if technology can be, it must be, and we should just accept that fact. That rationale does have a certain commonsense appeal.

For example, once computers became possible, they also became necessary. Living without them was not a viable option. We build nuclear bombs only because we think we must, not because we plan to use them. In time we will probably clone human beings as well, for no better reason than because we can.

But technology doesn't have a mind of its own, at least not yet. In any time and place, its power to dominate depends on how well it dovetails with popular goals, ambitions, and ideologies. The truly influential machines, such as the Internet, the cell phone, and the

PC, do more than reflect the dominant ideology. They inspire the creation and adoption of new ideologies, forcing a change in our understanding of how the world ought to work.

When that happens, you see something startling occur. When new technology and new ideology fit together perfectly, each reinforcing the other, the pace of change accelerates and the whole landscape can be abruptly altered.

It happened during the Renaissance, when the telescope, the microscope, and the creation of the scientific method accelerated the questioning of authority that marked that era. It happened again during the Industrial Revolution, when Darwinian theory emerged just in time to justify the rampages of a winner-take-all industrial capitalism.

In our own era, the cult of speed—of friction-free commerce, of impatience and instant gratification and on-time delivery and 24/7— has become the central organizing principle of modern society. Like its predecessors, it is a process created and fed by technology.

In such a world, it's hard for any one of us to reject or even restrain technology. To do so is to risk being left behind in the Darwinian dust, like the dodo bird and the saber-toothed tiger. Technology must be embraced; we must surrender to it wholeheartedly to reap its full benefits.

Of course, people have been complaining about the pace of change for a very long time. I recently saw Fellini's great movie *Roma*, a tribute to the lost Rome of his youth. In one scene, set sometime in the late 1930s, an old man complains that the people of Rome aren't real Romans anymore, that everyone is in far too much of a hurry. So maybe our own era is not as different as we might believe.

On the other hand, the old man may have had a point. I happened to be in Rome myself over Christmas of 2000, and on Christmas Eve my family and I walked down to St. Peter's Square to watch a decrepit but valiant Pope John Paul II deliver an outdoor Mass in a cold drizzle. I'm not a religious person, but it was a moving ritual, except for the young Italian woman right behind us, yakking loudly into her cell phone throughout the service.

Right then, in the very heart of Christendom, I said my Christmas Eve prayer of gratitude:

"Thank God she's not American."

The cell phone is a nice symbol for what I'm trying to talk about. It's an immensely convenient piece of equipment, but we haven't yet evolved a working etiquette for its use. We haven't dared to tame it, to force it to abide by the rules of civilized behavior. This tool, this mere servant, rudely interrupts our meetings, movies, conversations, and dinners, even our most somber religious services, yet for some reason we accept that intrusion as if we dare not confront this powerful barbarian in our midst.

A crying human toddler in a quiet restaurant wouldn't get that kind of tolerance. It would be disciplined and made to understand that such things just aren't done. But we forgive the cell phone for such intrusions because it plugs us into the body electric, makes us as one with the cast of millions also carrying cell phones everywhere they go, never out of touch, never unavailable.

The sense of connection is so sweet, so reassuring, that many have found it addicting. For them, the prospect of coming off the network, of losing contact, has become terrifying.

Just yesterday, when my plane landed at the Portland airport and finally taxied to the gate, a dozen or so people immediately whipped out their cell phones, frantic to reconnect. They had all the desperation of junkies who had been denied a fix for a few hours. In the rest room a few minutes later, the man standing at the next urinal had a cell phone tucked against his ear, chatting with his wife about how to juggle the family schedule.

And I read in the paper a while back about a hiker in the Olympic

Mountains, a couple of hundred miles northwest of here. Using his cell phone, he had called park rangers and told them to send a rescue helicopter.

"Are you hurt?" they asked.

No, not at all.

"Are you out of food? Are you lost?"

No, he had food and water, and thanks to his GPS device he could tell them exactly where they should come to pick him up. You see, he had this important meeting in Seattle that he needed to make. . . .

He didn't get his helicopter.

Over time, you come to recognize a pattern. We take a tool created to make life easier in some way—say, to give us more time—and instead we use it to make our lives more rushed. We introduce powerful tools into the culture and then we adapt ourselves to them, rather than force the machines to adapt to us. As Ralph Waldo Emerson described it, "Things are in the saddle, and ride mankind."

That's part of the explanation, I think, for the undercurrent of anxiety that flows through modern culture. Repeated surveys demonstrate a falling level of happiness even as material wealth has increased, a phenomenon that challenges the most basic assumptions of our capitalist society. We're all so busy multitasking, emulating the computer that has become the role model of a truly connected person, that we now experience life as a disconnected, incoherent accident.

It's as though the whole world has become an ecotone: all edge, competition and action; no center, calm and restoring.

When animals are confronted with such confusion, their instinct is to withdraw, to find a small place they can defend and remain there, hostile to any interlopers. I think if you look around these days, you'll see human beings responding much the same way, withdrawing emotionally, socially, physically, and intellectually into a smaller, more defensible place. Even small risks are magnified into enormous threats.

Maybe that's another reason that I treasure my annual escape to the Deschutes. The desert has always been a great place for contemplation. It may not hold the answers to our questions; those can be found only in our heads. At least the bits and pieces of them can. But out in the wild I find the time to fit those pieces together in new ways, to play around with the Rubik's Cube in my head until new patterns emerge.

Back in the real world, the barrage of data monopolizes our thoughts, keeping us skimming over the surface of things. Out here, the absence of outside distraction forces us to explore within, to go deeper. So over the next few days, as we fish and float and talk, I also want to explore what it's like to live in the dawn of the twenty-first century, to think a little more deeply about the forces we've put into play, and how best we might govern and benefit from them.

I turn to look out the window again. The miles are falling away quickly. We've turned off the main highway now and are making our way along a two-lane farm road through fields of sweet-smelling, impossibly green mint, adjoining fields of equally intense purple lavender, and straw-yellow wheat heavy with August grain. The colors are like something out of Van Gogh. This is a high desert plateau, but the fields are all irrigated with water pumped from the river below.

Richard comes to a stop sign, then makes a right turn. The road starts to drop quickly now, bringing us down off the plateau and through the little farming community of Gateway. We drive past the abandoned railroad station that looks like something out of a John Ford Western, then turn left onto a gravel road. The handful of homes here are small and well kept, but there's no sign of life. Everyone's either inside, taking shelter from the August heat, or out in the fields working.

On the other side of town we pass through ranchlands, with cattle scrounging among the sagebrush for a bit of grass or greenery. Then the road plunges down once again, this time into the canyon itself. The trailer behind us, laden with food and camping gear, begins to jostle and squeak on the suddenly rough road.

"It's time," I say to Richard, reaching over to slip a CD into the stereo mounted in his dashboard. A few seconds later, the first few power chords of ZZ Top fill the cabin. Richard's balding head begins to bob up and down in time to the music, like one of those rear-window Chihuahuas, and he turns to me with an idiot grin on his face, not saying a word.

My head starts bobbing too.

I turn around to see Alan finally looking up from his task, an idiot grin on his own face, not saying a word. Not that I could hear him anyway. Richard has turned the volume up full blast. Marv and Stewie are doing the Chihuahua in unison, augmented by air guitar. Talented boys, those two.

It may not seem so, but this is a carefully plotted ritual. Years ago, we discovered that if we began this particular CD at this particular moment of the trip, a miracle of convergence would occur. After another seventeen minutes of picking our way down this grade, the river is going to come into view. And at that moment, if we've timed it right, our favorite kick-ass song on the album will start to play. It's like having a sound track to our own private movie.

We pass under the old wooden railway trestle, which means that in a couple more turns of the road we'll be at the river. Off to the right is an abandoned settler's cabin, another landmark. And . . . there it is, just where it's always been, a deep blue ribbon of water streaming through a beige desert landscape. On the stereo the boys in ZZ Top come in right on cue, digging into a blowout guitar boogie called "La Grange."

"Budda-bum bum bum bum bum ba dum bum . . ."

The air guitars behind me kick into high gear. I decide to add drums to the action, gleefully pounding on the dashboard with my palms until I notice Richard giving me a dirty look. Gotta take care of that equipment, eh Dick?

A few minutes later, as we drive past the campground entrance, "La Grange" comes to an end. Before the next song can begin I hit eject on the CD player and return the disc to its case. The music was great, but ohhh, the silence is so much better. We roll down the windows and let the dry desert heat penetrate the manufactured coolness of the interior. All we can hear now is the bouncing of the trailer on the rough road.

And you can smell the river.

We pull off into our usual spot, overlooking the water. Tonight we'll camp here and get everything organized. Tomorrow morning we'll break camp at sunrise, reload the gear into the trailer, and climb back out of the canyon. The outfitter is meeting us at 10 A.M. at the launch site about eight miles upriver from here, where we'll trade the Yukon for two white-water rafts and an inflatable kayak.

There's the campsite. Richard hits the brakes, and four doors immediately fly open. To look at us, you'd think we'd never been here before. Each of us walks off into a private space and stares up into the sky, turning in little circles and trying to take it all in . . . the sound of the streaming water, the intense heat on shoulders and back, the strong scent rising out of the river and the sagebrush, the color of the sky and the canyon walls to the east, rising thousands of feet above us.

Alan straps on his fanny pack, bulging with lures and fishing gear, like John Wayne strapping on his six-shooter. Then he grabs his rod in one hand and a cold beer in the other, and announces that he's heading upstream to fish.

Richard takes that as a signal to go to work. He yanks his tent and sleeping bag out of the trailer and begins to set up camp. No fun for him until he has everything in order. Stewie starts rummaging through a cooler, looking for something to eat. Marv and I grab a couple of cold beers and head for the shade down by the river.

He and I have been close friends for twenty years now. We were born just a week apart, and each of us has two daughters, about the same ages. We both come from blue-collar backgrounds. My dad was an enlisted man in the air force; Marv's dad was a logger. Marv's funnier than I am, and also taller—the towheaded Big Swede played forward for his college basketball team.

On the other hand, I'm smarter and better looking. So things even out.

Overall, though, we're alike in so many ways that it only seems to heighten the ways in which we differ.

Take politics. I'm a good old-fashioned liberal, Marv's a Rush Limbaugh Republican, and we're usually not together long before we start getting into it. We're pretty equally matched—fighting out of the same weight class, so to speak—and we've had some long, heated debates that on occasion spiraled into something more. We're like two boys wrestling, constantly testing each other. It's how we communicate.

For the last few years, though, we've called a truce of sorts, particularly on the river. Well, not exactly a truce. More like a long-running, extended guerrilla war. We still ambush each other whenever we find the opportunity, but we're careful not to escalate beyond that.

But we can also just stand here together, watching the deep blue water run past us, seeing it sparkle in the late-afternoon sunshine, listening to the gurgle, and not say a word, feeling wonderfully comfortable, happy to be sharing the moment.

After a few minutes of aquatic communion, we turn without speaking and walk back up the bank toward the picnic table, where Stew and Richard are sitting. Richard, his tent now shipshape, is getting his gear ready for the evening fishing; Stewie is talking—about food as usual.

"So what are you cooking for dinner tonight?" Stew asks Richard, who on most evenings is also our designated chef.

"Chicken fajitas, Stew."

"With the onions and garlic? Did you remember to buy sour cream?"

"Yes we did, Stew."

"Salsa?"

"Yes."

"Great. I'll help. When do you want to start? You want me to help?"

Stew, to his credit, is also Richard's sous chef. He chops and dices and stirs and fetches, and generally stands at Richard's elbow, egging him on to culinary greatness and sneaking samples whenever he can.

"I'm going fishing first, Stew."

"Oh. Yeah. Okay."

I giggle, then sit down to start rigging my rod.

A half hour later, I'm hiking by myself on a trail along a steep bank, watching the river below for a good spot to fish. I've shucked my shirt and am down to a pair of shorts and my hiking boots. It's probably close to one hundred degrees out here, but the sun feels great on my back. You've got to watch where you're walking though . . . rattlesnakes abound out here.

So do grasshoppers, and many's the time I've stopped dead in my tracks, paralyzed with fear that I've heard a rattlesnake, only to discover that the noise came from grasshoppers jumping around in the dry brush. But you never dare assume it's not a snake. Better safe than sorry.

To my left, the sheer canyon wall rises perhaps a half mile into a clear blue sky. To my right, across the river, the land is more open, a sprawling desert of sagebrush dotted with a few scrub pines.

Both banks, though, are lined with green cottonwoods and alders and high grasses, living off the moisture of the river and providing shelter for fish and other wildlife. I hike along the trail, perched on the rim of a steep, rocky bank about thirty feet above the river, until I spot a place to fish.

It has everything: a nice rock to stand on; a slow, steady current below it where fish are likely to hold; and some casting room away from the trees. Perfect. Before I head down the incline, though, I roll a hand-sized rock down the slope, watching it bounce crazily all the way to the bottom.

You want to let the snakes know you're coming, so they can get out of the way.

Then, gingerly, I start picking my way down the bank. The footing's treacherous; you have to be careful.

A couple of minutes later, I'm ready to make my first cast. I'm not expecting to catch much here—the road access means that this place is fished pretty heavily compared to other areas. I just want to get a line wet, smell the water, feel the current, let my mind wander.

There's a rhythm to this river, a pace that joins your mind, body, and soul, and coming from the real world to this, it takes a little while to find it. It's not a steady beat; it's more of a pulse. When it pushes, you give; when it gives, you push. It's a dance, and the river has the lead. You have to just let it happen. If you fight it, if you insist on trying to set the pace, the river will wear you out. It's bigger and stronger than you are.

The opposite bank is reservation land, governed by the Warm Springs Confederated Tribes. It's beautiful country, but not good for much except looking at. Three tribes—the Wasco, the northern Paiute, and the Wallawalla—live together over there, about three thousand people in all. They run some cattle and operate a profitable timber business on reservation land farther west, where they still get enough rain for trees to grow. They also own a hotel-casino at the warm springs that give the reservation its name.

Of the three tribes, only the Paiute were traditionally desert dwellers—they lived originally in southeastern Oregon and Nevada. In settler accounts they were called Diggers because they lived mainly off roots. The two other tribes originally lived north of here, along the Columbia River. They were evicted from the rich farmlands along the river in 1855 and were exiled here.

The real blow came much later, though, well within living memory. Back in the early 1980s, when I was still working as a reporter in this area, an elder of the Wasco told me about the morning he watched his people's culture disappear. It is in some ways a dislocation like that experienced by many modern peoples, only compressed into the space of a few tragic hours.

His story began—and ended—at a place that no longer exists.

Every spring, salmon migrate from the Pacific up the Columbia River to spawn. Their numbers are smaller than they used to be, in the tens of thousands most years instead of the millions, but still they come. And until fairly recently, the salmon had to pause in their journey at a place called Celilo Falls.

Here the broad Columbia—judging from pictures, it was probably half a mile wide at that point—tumbled thirty feet in a misty, noisy tangle of small falls and rapids that extended all the way across the river. The migrating salmon would have to pause at the foot of those falls, gathering the strength to leap the obstacle in stages and resume their journey upstream to spawn.

The Wasco and other tribes along the river also congregated at the falls each spring, drawn by the salmon. At the height of the spawning migration, one fisherman, equipped with a long dip net and perched on rickety scaffolding extending out over the falls, could pull half a ton of rich salmon from the river in a single day. Such bounty made Celilo Falls the religious, social, and economic center of a multitribal culture that stretched up and down the river.

The falls were the most important trading spot in the pre-European West, drawing goods from as far as a thousand miles away.

In the spring of 1806, Meriwether Lewis and William Clark passed by Celilo on their way back home from the Oregon coast, and left the first recorded observation of the falls' importance.

"There was great joy with the natives last night," Lewis wrote in his journal April 19, "in consequence of the arrival of the Salmon; one of those fish was caught. . . . this fish was dressed and being divided into small peices was given to each child in the village, this custom is founded in a supersticious opinion that it will hasten the arrival of the Salmon."

Even back then, though, Lewis and Clark probably understood that they were witnessing a culture in decline. A few years earlier, trading ships landing at the mouth of the Columbia had brought smallpox to the Northwest, and even one hundred miles inland it had already begun wiping out entire villages. Eventually the disease would claim 50 percent or more of the native population.

And after the disease, and after the fur traders and explorers, came the settlers. Just fifty years after Lewis and Clark's arrival in the region, the few Wasco who had survived all that upheaval were removed altogether from their traditional homelands, evicted to make room for the tens of thousands of white people who had arrived via the Oregon Trail.

By treaty, the tribes did manage to retain the right to fish at their traditional spots at Celilo Falls, and with that right they also retained something of their cultural identity. Even today, the descendants of the Wasco return each spring to the Columbia to await the First Salmon, and they still perform the ceremonies marking the abundance it once heralded.

But the focus of their lives and culture, the falls, has disappeared.

In 1957, the federal government completed construction of the massive Dalles Dam a few miles downstream from Celilo Falls. Federal officials warned the tribes that once the dam gates were closed, the waters of the Columbia would back up, drowning Celilo Falls beneath a newly formed lake. The feds offered the tribes a financial settlement for their loss, a take-it-or-leave-it proposition.

The middle-aged man who told me this story was just a boy back then. As he remembered it, some of the Wasco had scoffed at the silliness of the white man who thought he could make the mighty Celilo disappear. On the appointed day for the gate closing, he stood alongside his father and other tribe members on a bluff overlooking the river, to watch what would happen.

First a whistle blew far downstream, to signal the closing of the gates. Then slowly, almost imperceptibly at first, the waters of the Columbia began to back up, climbing inch by inch up the concrete wall of the Dalles Dam, and inch by inch up the rocks and boulders of Celilo Falls.

Aghast, the older Wasco turned their backs on the river, refusing to witness the terrible event. But they could not close their ears, and as the river rose higher and higher behind them, they were forced to listen as the noisy rumble of living, falling water drowned beneath a placid silence.

It sounded to the Wasco like the silence of death. And then, my witness said, a wail of mourning came up out of his people.

He and others who knew Celilo intimately still speak of the falls as an amputee might speak of a lost leg. They still feel its existence, they still hear its roar, they still feel the spray upon their face. And—in a time frame longer than I'm trained to think in—I guess it does still exist, waiting beneath the domesticated waters of the Columbia, ready to emerge when the Dalles Dam washes away.

In the meantime, the Wasco have joined other tribes in trying to build another large gambling casino, this one a few miles downstream from their former fishing grounds. There they hope to win back at the blackjack tables some meager compensation for what the white man has taken from them.

That story haunts me, in part because of the grief I could hear in that man's voice thirty years after his loss. He mourned the destruction of the falls more deeply than if he had lost a loved one. People are meant to die, and somehow life continues after that loss. But the death of a culture is the death of a person's world. His people's story—the story that explained the world and their place in it—had abruptly ended, leaving them stranded out here in someone else's world, someone else's story. It had made them an orphan people.

Yet until the arrival of Lewis and Clark, it all must have seemed so permanent to the Wasco. What power on earth could stop the salmon from returning? What could destroy something as mighty as the falls?

They could not envision a culture enamored with the process of creative destruction, a culture organized not around a falls or religion or ethnic identity or even a way of life, but around change itself.

I bring my line in and try another cast. Even though the real fishing doesn't begin until after we pick up the boats, I'd still love to hook up with something tonight, just to feel that sensation of something wild and desperate on the other end of my line.

But once again, nothing.

I look up at the sky, trying to gauge the time. If I want to make it back to camp by dark, I've probably got another half hour to fish. Time to implement the three-cast rule: If you make three casts in the same hole without catching anything, move on.

I reach back, ready to fling the lure as far out into the river as I can for the final cast in this spot. The lure splashes, then swings down into the current, tugging gently. I wait, and wait, and wait . . . nothing.

Ah well.

Across the river, about a hundred feet away, an osprey cruises along the bank, looking to snag a trout rising to the surface for the evening insect hatch. He's a lot more serious about it than I am, and he should be; he's fishing for survival, not sport.

I reel the line in, then pick my way back up the steep bank to the trail. By the time I reach the top I'm breathing heavily and my legs ache. I'm not in river shape yet. By the end of the week, I'll make a climb like that without a problem, but today it's a struggle.

It's tempting to say that the canyon never changes, that here at least is something eternal. But even that's not true. The water level changes a lot from year to year, which can alter the whole character of the river. It means that a spot that's productive one year might be barren the next. Rocks that are submerged in a high-water year become serious obstacles for a raft at low water. Sometimes the streambed will shift, taking out a whole line of trees along the bank.

A few years ago, a huge spring flood really changed things. Even today, you can look twenty feet up in the trees along the river and see logs and other debris deposited there by the high water.

And, of course, the five of us change from year to year too. Ten years ago we were all in our twenties and early thirties, and we tackled the river like fools too stupid to know we could get hurt. Time and the river have made us a little wiser about that.

The outside world intrudes here as well. Richard's wife left him last spring, moved in with another guy from her office. And while he has sounded okay on the phone in recent months, I can already tell he hasn't gotten over it. He's always had a prickly side to him, a gruff sort of defensiveness that can make him come off like an asshole to some people. Now he's turned that up a notch, and I can't say I blame him. I guess it's like a rock that appears in low water— we're just gonna have to steer around that one this year.

Those kinds of changes, though, are part of being human, part of being friends. We come equipped to handle them. It's changes of a different sort that I wonder about.

We live these days in a world that is remade continually, hour by hour, even as we sleep. But there's no single event that epitomizes that change. There's seldom a dramatic moment in which a whistle blows to announce that the world is now different. The attacks of September 11 were such a moment, I guess, but they are rare. And in hindsight, even that sudden event now seems like the culmination of changes that had long been under way, but had simply not been noticed yet.

As Americans, we've gotten pretty used to that constant change. This country was founded by people who sought to transform themselves and the world, and throughout our relatively short national existence we've become the world's primary agent of social, economic, political, and technological change. We excel both at creating change and at living with its consequences.

But I wonder why we excel. What makes us capable of absorbing change at a pace other cultures cannot handle?

I think it's because those facets of a society that inhibit chaos in other cultures—a sense of obligation to community, loyalty to tradition, a strong social structure—either never developed or were tossed aside as impediments here in the United States.

So if, as Americans, we awake each morning and remake the world anew, we also awake each morning to a strange world, unfamiliar and disquieting. If severing ties to community has made us flexible, able to respond quickly to the demands of economy and society, it has also isolated us from the comfort and security that family and community have long provided our species.

If accelerating the pace of change has made us more productive, creating material affluence, that pace has also rendered us confused and our value systems archaic and unenforceable. It has left us poorer, in the sense that we have lost the ability to measure human worth in any way but dollar signs.

The fact that we have grown accustomed to feeling disoriented, uprooted in time as well as place, doesn't make that disorientation any less important. By pursuing technological prowess, we have all but freed ourselves from the randomness of nature. But in doing so, we have courted an artificial chaos against which we offer little defense.

In fact, if peace of mind is a rare commodity in this new world, it's by design. We might be surrounded by material goods, by signs of affluence and plenty, but for the most part we're not comfortable. Inner peace, because it cannot carry a price tag or bar code, is not a commodity highly valued in a consumer culture.

The day is getting on; in the last five minutes the sun has dropped below the western horizon and left me standing in the shadows. Darkness is coming. In about twenty minutes it will engulf the whole canyon. I need to find one more spot to fish.

"Yo, bro, catch anything?"

I turn to see Alan clambering up the bank behind me. He had been upstream, hidden by the trees just a hundred yards away.

"Nah. Just chucking it out there. How about you?"

"Not a thing. I'm heading back to camp. You staying?"

I stop to think. Let's see: He hasn't caught anything either, so there's no shame in going back empty-handed.

"No. I'm ready. I just wanted to get my line in water anyway."

Fifteen minutes later we walk back into camp. Stewie and Richard are at the crude wooden picnic table, carving up vegetables and chicken breasts, getting dinner ready. Marv sits at the other end of the table, with a Marlboro Light in one hand and a Scotch on the rocks in the other. Laid out in front of him is a backgammon board, the pieces all prepared for a game.

He looks like a three-card monte artist, waiting for a sucker to walk by.

"Where the hell did that come from?" I say, pointing down to the backgammon board.

"Oh, I picked it up a few days ago. Thought it might be fun out here on the river," Marv says, a smug look on his face. "Either of you Bookman brothers care to play, quarter a point? Winner stays, loser walks. Best two out of three."

This is something new. We've never brought games on the river, not even a deck of cards. It's just something we never thought of, I guess.

"You're toast," Alan says eagerly, setting his fishing pole down and unbuckling his fanny pack from his waist. "Let me get a beer."

Marv grins, happy to have a victim. I know he plays a lot of backgammon, and I know he thinks he's pretty good. I know that because he thinks he's good at everything. On the other hand, while I know the game, I don't know it well. It's not something that Alan and I played as kids.

I set down my pole, unsnap my own fanny pack, and then walk over to the trailer, looking for my equipment. Now that the sun's down it'll be dark soon. I want to set up my gear while I can still see.

I pull my backpack, my sleeping bag, and a large lime green tarp out of the pile of equipment. Alan and I always sleep out on the tarp, under the stars. Marv and Richard—the Republicans, we call them—usually sleep in their own tents. You might call Stewie the swing voter in the crowd. Sometimes he'll sleep outside with us Democrats; sometimes he prefers to sleep indoors, in the Gore-Tex suburbs.

I hump my gear toward the river, looking for a flat place to spread the tarp. Over at the picnic table, I hear Marv cry out in mock pain. Evidently Alan is putting a hurting on him at the backgammon board.

Excellent.

A couple of hours later, darkness has fallen, the stars are beginning to pop out, and the temperature is falling fast. A fifty-degree swing from daytime to nighttime is pretty common out here, so we've all changed into pants and long-sleeved shirts. By later in the evening we'll have added sweatshirts or jackets.

The smell of sautéed onions and Mexican spices still hangs heavy in the night air. Richard and Stewie have served us a marvelous dinner, and in the darkness we can hear Stewie somewhere over by the stove, trying to scavenge a last fajita. Everybody's had a few beers by now, and laughter is easily provoked. We've made the transition.

Alan is over at the tarp, rolling out his sleeping bag and setting up for the night by flashlight. He didn't have a chance to tend to his housekeeping earlier because a long winning streak kept him at the backgammon board until dinner. He took two straight games from Marv, then won two out of three from both me and Stewie before beating Marv again two straight.

And let me tell you, Marv is not happy about it. To his mind, a great injustice has been done. The earth is out of balance, and he will not rest easy until it has been restored.

He and I and Richard are sitting in a circle near the riverbank, a small propane lantern in the center lighting our faces. It's illegal to have a campfire: They're banned in the canyon this time of year because the danger of a range fire is so high.

"So how much do I owe you?" Marv asks as Alan walks out of the darkness and back into the circle of light.

"Six seventy-five," Alan says, a tight, smug smile apparent on his face even in the dim light.

It's not the money that matters; it's money as a way of keeping score. And at a quarter a point, Alan has clearly established backgammon dominance. As Ken Kesey would say, he's the bull goose loony, for tonight anyway.

"You know we're playing again tomorrow, don't you?" Marv tells Alan. "That luck of yours can't last the whole trip. By the end I'm gonna be kicking your butt."

Alan takes a seat and is about to respond when he's interrupted by a loud yelp. Peering into the darkness, we see a panicked Stewart hustling back our way, eyes sparkling in the lantern light.

"Skunks!" he hisses as he comes our way, plate in hand. "There's two of them . . . big as damn Dobermans."

The talking stops, and in the sudden silence we can hear them, rustling around the stove and the food boxes, vague shapes moving in the darkness.

"Hey! Get out of there!" Marv yells, his insistence halfhearted at best. Richard and I rise out of our seats, starting to move toward the food. I pick up the lantern and Richard stomps his feet, hoping the noise will frighten them off.

It doesn't. Instead, one of the skunks comes ambling toward us as casual and confident as a cop walking his beat.

My God. Stewart was right. The thing's huge.

I set the lantern down, and we sit silently back in our seats, chastened and afraid to move. The second skunk, almost as big as the first, follows his partner into the light. Sniffing along the ground, seemingly oblivious of our presence, they march right into our circle.

Marv, ever the instigator, draws his long legs up out of the way and begins to giggle loudly.

"Shut up! Don't scare them, you jerk!"

"Where'd they go? Oh God. Where's the other one?"

"They're huge!"

"Jay!" whispers Stewart, who has taken a seat right next to me. "I think one of 'em's right under my chair. Ahhwww! He's . . . touching my leg! Oh man. I gotta get out of here."

I look down and to my left. The skunk has found Stewart's plate on the ground. His snout is in the food, and in the lamplight I can see his uplifted tail pointed right back up at me, about two feet from my face.

It's like looking down the barrel of a loaded shotgun.

I'm not proud. I start to beg.

"Stewart . . . Please, please don't you dare move, Stewart, he's right there. I'm a dead man if you move."

Stewart doesn't move. But then the absurdity of the situation hits him, and like Marv he too starts to laugh. As he does, his chair begins to shake beneath him.

"Oh man, the other one's over here! Look! What's he doing?"

I glance away from my impending doom to see Richard, on the other side of the circle, stand up slowly and back away into the dark. The rest of us, though, are still frozen in our chairs.

"What do we do?"

"Oh my God. Oh my God."

"Watch out, he's coming your way now!"

"Hey guys, I'm gonna throw a rock at him," teases Richard, now hidden from view in the darkness behind us and safely out of skunk range.

"If you do, I'll kill you, you asshole."

Giggles become helpless laughter, but the skunks, thank God, don't seem fazed by any of it. They simply go about their business. We watch as the bigger one, his eyes fixed on us, starts backing away toward the darkness, dragging with him the remains of Stewart's last fajita. He pauses en route to take a substantial bite of his plunder.

Suddenly the skunk snorts, backs quickly away, and shakes his head violently from side to side, like a fish with a hook in its jaw, or someone who just inhaled a noseful of black pepper.

"Chili peppers got him!" yells Stew. "Yes! Serves you right, you food-stealing bastard!"

The skunk pauses, shakes his head, and snorts one more time, then disappears, sneezing as he goes. His buddy, however, has wandered back to the cooking area, and we can hear him in the darkness, rustling through the bags. Something heavy and metal crashes to the ground. Lord knows what he's gotten into now.

A couple of us stand, our courage returning. Somebody picks up a rock and tosses it toward the sound. The rustling stops, then resumes.

"Who's got a flashlight?"

"Here's one."

"Point it at him. Right over there. Yeah. There he is."

The skunk looks up into the light, eyes shining red, then slowly turns and trundles away.

"Anybody see his friend?"

"I think he's gone too. I saw him going toward the river. Probably needs a drink."

"Him and me both."

"Did you see those things? I can't believe they did that!"

" 'Bigger than Dobermans,' you said. That is hilarious, Stewart."

"I told you they were bigger than Dobermans! Did you see 'em? Food-stealing bastards."

Gingerly, flashlights and lanterns lighting the way, we make our way over to the picnic table and the food supplies to assess the damage. The large frying pan that Richard used to cook the chicken strips has been knocked to the ground—that must have been the noise we heard.

"Look, there's what's left of your fajita, Stewart," Marv says, shining his light on a half-eaten piece of chicken breast lying on the ground.

"He's like my ex-wife," Richard says, staring at the chicken. "She didn't like my cooking either."

"I think they even use the same perfume," says Marv quietly. "Wife-stealing bastard."

I think Richard smiles, but in the darkness I can't be sure. It certainly ends the banter. Silently, we set to work cleaning up the mess and washing the dishes, trying to remove anything that might attract another visit. At Richard's direction, we stow the trash and the rest of the food safe inside the Yukon. By the time the camp is put back together, the excitement of our uninvited guests has worn off and everybody's ready for bed.

Stewart had been planning to sleep out on the tarp with Alan and me, but the skunks have spooked him into going Republican. He pulls out his tent and sets it up about twenty feet away from us, then says good night and zips himself inside.

I have to admit, I'm a little nervous myself about sleeping under the stars. But in the end, weighing the slight possibility of another visit from the skunks against the certainty that Alan and I would get teased unmercifully if we put up our tents, we decide to brave it, as manly Democrats should.

Besides, once we're snug in our sleeping bags, staring up into the bowl of stars over our heads and watching meteors streak across the sky, any fear we might have felt disappears. It's good to be back.

day two

The river is cold, so cold that the first step into the water makes your heart stop and your head pound. Your legs go numb, and then the pain sets in, so intense and fiery that it strips your mind of any thought but escape.

Then, just as you're about to give in—just when you're ready to splash back to shore in humiliating, abject panic—the pain subsides a bit. It's still damn cold . . . shit it's cold! . . . but you can tolerate it.

Barely.

I'm standing next to our raft, loading equipment. Stewie, still standing dry and warm up on the bank, grins at my discomfort, then tosses me a heavy rubber river bag filled with equipment. I brace to absorb its weight, catch it, then swing it over to the back of our fourteen-foot inflatable raft. Another waterproof bag, then another and another. You always want to load the heavy stuff first, to keep your center of gravity as low as possible. Crashing through rapids with a top-heavy raft is not recommended.

After the heavy equipment, you load the river bags crammed with sleeping bags and clothing, again sealed tight against the water.

The last to be loaded are the food bags, so they're not crushed under the weight of tents and other equipment. Then, once everything's on board, the stack of bags is strapped down tight to the raft's aluminum frame.

Oh. Did I mention lounge chairs?

Probably not. They undercut the image we seek of macho men about to embark on a dangerous backcountry rafting trip. But a few years back, one of our number had the genius—the courage, really—to smuggle a folding lounge chair onto his raft. Once we discovered his crime, we used the opportunity to rib him cruelly as the wimp he had proved himself to be.

Then, for the next six days, while the rest of us perched our sore butts on rocks or stumps each evening in camp, the genius (okay, it was Marv) reclined in regal and extremely aggravating luxury. Whenever he left camp to fish, the rest of us fought like eight-year-olds for his chair, and chairs have been standard equipment ever since. At the end of a long day on the river, it's the very height of elegance to lie back in a recliner and watch the shooting stars lay trails of phosphorescence across the black desert sky.

After the river bags and chairs are loaded, Stewie and I grab one of the coolers, brimming with ice and beer and food, and wrestle it into place at the center of the raft, where it can also double as a rowing bench.

We load a second large cooler as well, this one filled with nothing but big blocks of ice. It's been sealed shut with duct tape, and when we cut it open on the third or fourth day out, the ice will still be fresh enough to last the rest of the trip.

Once the coolers are packed, we begin to stow the fishing equipment, the rods and reels and tackle boxes. Loading is hard work, but in the dry desert air it's impossible to work up a sweat. Any moisture evaporates the moment it leaves your pores.

When I finally glance up from our labor, I see Marv and Alan hefting their own cooler into place. Richard, his gear already loaded, is snapping on a life preserver; he'll be riding in the kayak today.

"Got your fishing vest this year, Richard?"

He stares at me, wordlessly.

I stand and stretch, my eyes taking in the pale blue cloudless sky, the dark blue Deschutes flowing in front of me, the light tan desert baking under a brilliant sun, the snowcapped Mount Jefferson off in the distance.

This is what I've anticipated on those dark winter days, in those hours spent in a cubicle beneath fluorescent lights, struggling with computers and voice mail and e-mail and meetings. I want to hit the pause button, to make time stand still, to make this sweet instant linger awhile.

"Man, I'm glad that part's finished," Stew says. "Time for a beer?" I smile and nod. He reaches into the cooler and pulls out two cans.

We've been packing for about an hour, and the morning coolness has faded under the intense sun. By now, both of us are standing thigh-deep in the river, and the contrast between the cold water running past my legs and the heat on my bare back feels sensuous, almost overwhelming my nervous system. Every nerve cell in my body has been activated, sending signals to the central processing unit. And every message is the same: "Man, this feels so damn good."

I crack open my beer and take a long cold swallow. Stewie sets his beer on the raft bench and unties the bow rope from a nearby tree.

"Ready to shove off?" I say.

Stew breaks out into that wide grin.

"Ohhhhh yeah," he says.

I laugh and climb aboard, take up the two oars, and shift my weight until I find a good rowing position. Stew, still on shore, places his palms on the raft and braces his legs against the bank. He's a powerful man, about five ten and something over two hundred pounds. He played a lot of rugby back in high school and college, and even now it wouldn't be any fun to see him coming at you on a football field, knowing you had to take him on.

"You say when," he tells me, like an overgrown kid at the dinner table, waiting for permission to dig in.

I glance over to our buddies; they look about ready too.

"Now's good."

With a grunt, Stew scrapes us off the river bottom and out into the current. Once we're floating free of the shore he gives us a final shove and then launches himself headfirst into the raft, arms and legs flying.

As Stew struggles to right himself, I pull hard at the oars, to get us out into the mainstream, away from land. Once clear, I push forward on the left oar and pull back on the right, putting the raft into a half spin until I can see the other guys behind us—Richard sitting low in the kayak, Alan and Marv in the raft. They too hit the current and are swept quickly downstream, coming up alongside us. For a few moments the three craft bob together in the middle of the river, everyone smiling, joking, a little giddy at finally getting under way.

Then we separate as we float through the first little riffle, just above the bridge on Highway 26.

As always, my exhilaration at beginning the trip is undercut by a sharp note of melancholy. It hits me every time, right about here, because I know it will be another long year before I once again stand at the beginning.

But I guess I should cheer up; this is the last we'll see of a paved road for a while. Five days of freedom ahead.

Out here on the river, the smell of clean, fresh water fills your nostrils, and the sound of its flow fills your ears. Most of the water comes from snowmelt off the east side of the Cascades, so it's pure and blue-clear.

But that's not really why it's so cold. The water stays frigid—and running high even now, in the desert heat and drought of August—because it gurgles up from the bottom of Lake Simtustus, a man-made lake created by a dam a couple of miles upstream from our launch spot.

Without Pelton Dam, which produces electricity and stores water for irrigation, the Deschutes would be a warmer, more seasonal flow and could not support a blue-ribbon trout fishery. As an environmentalist, I'm supposed to want to tear down the western dams, and where that's feasible it ought to be done . . . in most cases. But I have to be honest: If they ever breached Pelton Dam, restoring the Deschutes to its natural state, it would ruin a damn fine trout river and break my heart in the process.

For the first couple of miles we float through a portion of the river still accessible by dirt road. The river feels young here, immature and almost frisky. There's not much work required to floating this section. Once in a while I drop the oars into the water, just to keep us riding in the middle of the channel and away from the overhanging trees along the bank. But for the most part I'm just taking in the sights.

The fishing is probably pretty good through this early stretch of river, but we've never tried it. To our minds it's tainted by its proximity to asphalt. The boats make us snobs; we wish them to carry us places where the foot-bound hoi polloi cannot easily follow.

Besides, it's so pleasant to be back on the river again, just floating along. No one wants to stop so soon after getting under way.

Both banks through here are lush and green with vegetation. Slender alders and high cottonwoods crowd the shore for space, and tall grass and reeds fill any gap left by the trees. Just a few feet back from the waterline, though, the desert is once again harsh and bare, dotted with hardy, pungent sagebrush. On a hot, still day, you can walk by a particularly aromatic sagebrush and it's like walking past the perfume counter at the mall Macy's.

Over to the right, an ancient two-rutted road snakes down the steep canyon wall, where horse-drawn wagons used to bring supplies from the upper plateau down to the reservation. It's probably been a hundred years since anyone used the road, but the desert heals slowly. It's easy to imagine the teamsters trying to manage a team of horses as they—

"Look," Stew says, startling me out of my reverie. He points ahead to the right bank, where Alan and Marv have pulled their boat into a nice fishing spot. Richard is nowhere in sight: He must be somewhere ahead of us in the kayak.

"Any luck?" I ask as we float past.

"Just got here," says Alan, flipping his lure into the water.

He's my brother. He doesn't say much.

But the ice is broken. The fishing frenzy has hit early this year.

I touch the oars to get us centered in the main current, then reach for my fishing rod to check the line, the knots, the setup. Stew does the same. We're ready to go.

There are a lot of special regulations for fishing the Deschutes, all designed for the fish's protection. For example, you can only use artificial lures, no bait. That would be too easy. You also have to release most of the fish you catch, so that the trout get a chance to reproduce. By regulation, you can keep only two small fish a day, and on most days we don't keep any at all.

You also can't fish from the boat—you have to be standing on the shore or in the water, which means that large parts of the river haven't been legally fished for decades. For the most part, the reservation side of the river is also off-limits to us. So from here on down, we'll keep a close eye on the right riverbank, looking for a good spot to beach the boat and fish.

The river here is probably about seventy feet wide, and a lot of water moves through it. Fishing a river this big and strong is a lot like hunting. At different times of day the fish will be hanging out in different parts of the river. To catch them you have to find them; you have to know what their habits are, where they're likely to be lurking.

The bigger fish are smart; they don't hold in the fast-running water, where they'd have to expend a lot of energy just to maintain position. They'll find a spot where they have some shelter from the current and then wait there, barely moving at all, until the faster water washes something tasty by them—a bug, or maybe a grasshopper blown into the river.

Then, with a flick of a tail, they'll slide into the current to pick it up, and then swing back into the calmer holding spot. It's as if they're eating at an aquatic dim sum restaurant, lounging patiently, then grabbing something appetizing as the cart goes by.

"How about we try right up there?" Stew says, pointing to an open spot on the right bank about a quarter mile downstream. I nod, and start pulling on the oars, getting us into position to land. These rafts are big and slow—you can't exactly turn them on a dime. Stew grabs the bow rope and moves to the front of the raft, ready to leap ashore and beach us once we get close to the bank.

A few minutes later, I'm standing bare-legged in the cold water again, this time casting into the river. The lure hits with a splash directly across from me, then catches in the current and sweeps downstream in a gentle arc. I can feel it vibrating through my rod. Just as the lure is about to pass from swift water into the slower current near the bank—pop!—the rod jerks in my hand and a nice strong rainbow erupts in a fountain of water about thirty feet downstream.

"Fish on!" I yell.

"Oh come on . . . already?" I hear Stew say in disbelief. We can't see each other; he's around the bend somewhere. But apparently he can hear me.

"First cast, man! He's big too . . . big as a Doberman!"

When you get a hookup like this, it's as if you're connected to the river itself. The fish is mostly unseen, but through your rod you can feel its power, its wildness, its surging desperation.

After a few minutes of struggle I bring the fish to me, slip a hand beneath his body, and, using a pair of pliers, gently disengage the hook from his mouth. It's a gorgeous rainbow, about fifteen inches long, its skin a glistening deep red from the rich insect life in the river. Then, still cradling the fish in my hand, I slide him back and forth in the river, forcing oxygen-bearing water through his gills to revive him. Once his strength returns, he darts away out of my hand, back into the secret river.

Excited, I try a few more casts back at that spot, but nothing happens. The hole's gone dry. I turn and trudge out of the water toward shore, concentrating hard to ensure that my cold-numbed legs don't slip on the moss-covered rocks. Stew's still upstream, out of sight. That's okay; we're not in any hurry. I stand there, soaking up the sunshine and the sounds, the sips and gurgles of deep water passing swiftly by. A few minutes later, I hear Stew crashing through the underbrush toward the boat. He is not what you'd call a subtle person. Any rattlesnakes in the vicinity must be in the next county by now.

"Get anything?"

"Nah. How big was yours?"

"About fifteen inches. I thought I might get more in that spot, but that was it."

We get ready to shove off again, but as we look up we see Marv and Alan, floating our way. It looks as if they're pulling over to talk.

I glance at Stew, because we both know what must be coming. Ordinarily they'd float right on by, trying to beat us to the next good spot downriver. The only reason they'd be pulling over is if one of these guys caught a big fish, and they're stopping to brag about it.

Sure enough. Before their raft even touches shore, Alan asks the standard opening question.

"So . . . catch any?"

Stew says nothing, stubbornly refusing to take the lure Alan has thrown our way. But what the hell, I think. Let them have their fun.

"I caught a nice one, about fifteen inches, right down there," I say. "How about you guys?"

"Marv caught a big one already, nineteen inches," Alan says.

"Just a shade under twenty, actually," says Marv.

"Nineteen," Alan insists, looking hard at Marv. "But apparently it's still growing."

All eyes turn to Marv, who turns his head and stares back up the river, a big happy smile on his face. If he had a tail, it would be wagging so hard he'd beat himself to death.

I can see his mind turning. He's been mentally rehearsing his speech.

"Yup," he finally says, taking a drag on his ever-present cigarette just to draw out his moment. "Jumped three times, almost blocked out the sun it was so big. Took me ten minutes to haul him in. Felt like I had me a big dog on the other end of that line."

"Kinda like a Doberman?" I ask.

Marv's smile gets a little bigger.

"Exactly, J-Book. Eggs-actly like a Doberman. And after I let him go, I caught three more in the same spot. Four casts, four fish."

He looks back out at the river. "Caught 'em right below that big island back there, on a Hotshot," he says. "I think that works pretty good."

Marv's a salesman by trade, and a damned good one. He talks so sweetly he can charm a fish right out of the river. Every once in a while, if he gets lucky, he can even catch one with a fishing rod.

He may be right, though. Fishing below an island may be great strategy. If you catch a nice fish by working a certain lure in a certain type of water at a certain time of day—say, "right below that big island back there, on a Hotshot"—a smart fisherman is going to gnaw on that story, trying to extract its marrow:

"Maybe I caught a fish there because in the heat of the afternoon the big ones hang out in the riffles below islands, where there would be a lot of oxygen in the water. And maybe it attacked out of anger, because it saw the lure as a competitor intruding on its territory."

Armed with your hypothesis, you try it again below the next big island, to see if it produces the same outcome. If it does, if you catch fish in the riffle below that second island as well, maybe you've figured something out about that strange aquatic world.

It's the process we humans apply to everything, not just fishing. We're always trying to connect the dots, trying to discover the causes of certain effects, the effects of certain causes. In fact, as we try to puzzle out how we interact with the modern world around us, I think it's important to begin here, at the basic level of how we perceive and comprehend things.

For example, the defining, iconic image of our era is no doubt etched in the minds of all of us: the collapse of the World Trade Center towers on September 11, 2001. Months after that event, we discovered that U.S. intelligence agencies had possessed the raw data that might have allowed them to anticipate that attack. Unfortunately, those clues had been buried in megabytes, gigabytes, terabytes of less important data collected by spy satellites, communications intercepts, financial transactions, agent observations, interrogation transcripts, etc. Our intelligence agencies had been so overwhelmed with the data they had been collecting that uncounted hours of intercepted phone conversations among suspected terrorists had never even been translated out of Arabic into English.

Yet, in the wake of 9/11, the instinctive reaction of those intelligence communities was to seek still more intelligence data, as if a shortage of information had been the problem.

That betrays, I believe, a central fallacy of the modern era: If we fail to understand, more data will illuminate us. If still we fail to understand, still more data must be acquired. Eventually, as we follow that course to its natural conclusion, we reach a point at which our powers of conscious comprehension are overwhelmed and cease to operate. At that point we become mere receptacles for information, unable to process it intelligently, capable only of responding at the most primitive of levels.

But I'm getting a bit ahead of myself. Let's start at the most basic level of human comprehension. In Marv's case, he had acquired two facts: He was fishing below an island, and he caught a big one. It was certainly possible to think of those two facts as independent of each other: Event A and Event B, so to speak. If you say it that way— "Events A and B"—you have a mere listing of facts that doesn't tell you a damn thing.

But Marv, being more or less human, instinctively tried to tie the events together to make a story, connecting them as "Event A, then Event B." He was fishing below an island, *then* caught a big fish. As playwrights and novelists know, a helluva lot of drama can be packed into that little word "then."

And of all human activities, fishing in particular lends itself well to storytelling. You've heard the jokes: No fish is bigger than the one that got away; there are honest men, and fishermen, but no honest fishermen. In fact, some of our best writers have been fishermen. Hemingway wrote a lot of fish stories, from the Nick Adams short stories in his early days through *The Old Man and the Sea* toward the end. Melville wrote the biggest fish story of all time, even though, technically, it was about a mammal. And that one too got away in the end.

Maybe that tendency toward story is genetic, a product of evolution. Maybe our male ancestors improved their chances of procreating with some hot tribal babe by boasting about their hunting and fishing exploits each night around the campfire. Fishing and hunting stories would probably have been the ur-tales, the origins of narrative fiction and nonfiction.

Fishing and writing are similar in mind-set as well. To a fisher-man, the world beneath the water is a place you can enter only through your imagination. You may try to guess what's going on down there, but the only way to confirm or refute your guesswork is to toss in a lure and see what happens.

Like the fisherman, the writer can't see his audience. But like a fisherman, you try to give them something that looks close enough to real life to provoke the response you want.

Some of the pioneering work in human perception was per-formed in the early twentieth century by a young Czech psycholo-gist named Max Wertheimer, who went on to found Gestalt psychology. In one early experiment, Wertheimer and his colleagues put two small lightbulbs on a tabletop, wired so they would light in rapid sequence. The first bulb would light up, then go out just as the second bulb lit up.

Wertheimer found that if enough time separated the lighting of the two bulbs, a human subject saw them for what they were, as two distinct and independent events: Event A and Event B, so to speak.

But if the time between the lighting of the bulbs was reduced a bit, something remarkable happened. Wertheimer's human subjects now told him that they could see a blur of light travel across the tabletop from one bulb to another.

Of course, that blur of light didn't exist. The human mind invented it subconsciously to explain how the light "moved" from one bulb to another. It was the "then" needed to create a story, "A, then B."

Brain researchers today report a similar phenomenon. When they physically stimulate the part of the brain that produces laughter, for instance, their human subject will invariably insist that she laughed because she had seen or thought of something funny. The mind automatically invents that story to account for what happened.

More than fifty years after Wertheimer's initial work, experi-menters added a complication to what had become known as the "phi phenomenon." What would happen if you used lightbulbs of different colors? Would that destroy the illusion?

Nope.

It turned out that the human mind still saw the path of light moving between the bulbs—the blur simply appeared to change color halfway across. In other words, when the facts get more complex, the story we create becomes more complex to account for it.

Marv's story, I can tell, is about to get more complex as well. Give this man a stage and he will fill it. He takes another draw on his cigarette and is about to launch into the part of the story about how, against incredible odds, he was able to bring the giant fish to hand. But that puff on his cigarette, that pause in his story, gives me the opening I need. I jump to take it.

"So, how about you, Alan?" I ask. "Do any good?"

"No, nothing so far," Alan says. "A few hits, but nothing landed." My question, though, has just the impact that I had hoped.

"C'mon, Marv, time to go," he says. "You got your twenty-two-incher, there's one out there with my name on it too."

Marv would clearly like to brag a few minutes longer, but Alan has the oars. Stewie quickly steps forward to shove them off, and Alan pulls backward until the current grabs the raft and they slip silently downstream.

"Good move," I tell Stewie as we both stand there waving good-bye, and he laughs.

We stow our rods on board and get ready to shove off as well. By the time we get back out into the current, Alan and Marv have already pulled to the bank again, just a few hundred yards downstream.

It's as I suspected. My little brother doesn't like being outfished by his partner. He's eager to get a lure back in the water.

With his casual, gentle style and his long hair tied up in a pony-tail, Alan doesn't come across at first as someone who is highly competent, disciplined, and grimly competitive, someone who will grind you down into the dust if that's what it takes. As his older brother, I've known that about him for a long time, but it took these guys a year or two to find it out for themselves.

Then, once you've penetrated that level with him, the tendency is to think of him as imperturbable, to accept that placid, quiet surface he projects as a reflection of his inner self. And I don't think it is. I think he works hard at it, or at least he did at first. Now that he's reached forty—is still a bachelor, still living by himself—what was once facade is in some ways becoming fact. As Marv would say, he didn't get that way overnight.

Part of that reserve may come from our upbringing, which means I share it. Dad was a career enlisted man in the U.S. Air Force, and we grew up trailing him around the world as he was transferred every couple of years to a new assignment. Alan was the youngest of us three kids, and in our family he's known as Boose, as in caboose, as in the last railcar in the train.

It's a different way to grow up, always being the new kid, knowing that you could come home from school on any given day and be told to start packing to move across the country, or to a new country altogether.

When I left home for good, Alan was just fourteen. And because Dad was stationed in Europe at the time, and I had to stay Stateside to work during the summers, I never went home, not even for summers. For the next ten years or so, Alan and I saw each other only briefly, and we didn't really reconnect until we were both out of college.

Today, Boose still knows me in ways that no one else does. He's part of what connects the adult I am now to that shy adolescent of thirty years ago, to that little boy who was very much in awe of our father in his dark blue uniform with the sergeant's stripes. Alan has shared my story line, and there's really no substitute for that.

When we get to swapping family stories, though, it's amazing how much our memories will differ. Even though he was younger, he'll recall incidents that I have no memory of whatsoever. At other times, our memories will directly contradict each other, as if we had experienced two different childhoods.

That used to make me shake my head, until I ran across some research into memory by Daniel Offer, a psychiatrist at Northwestern University.

Back in 1962, Offer had interviewed seventy-three high school freshmen, asking them questions about their family life. In 1996, he tracked down and talked to sixty-seven of those boys, who were now forty-eight-year-old men. Offer found that the men did no better than chance in answering questions about their childhood. On many questions, in fact, an active form of forgetting seemed at work.

As young teenagers, 82 percent of the boys had said their parents disciplined them with physical punishment. As adults, only 33 percent of the men could recall being spanked or hit. That memory didn't fit their concept of who they had become, or what their childhood had been, so it was edited away. They subconsciously erased some dots, and created new ones, to give their lives the meaning they needed.

I guess I've done the same, in ways I'll never know, and Alan probably has too.

Stewie and I stop to fish at several more spots, and I do pretty well. I've caught and released half a dozen more fish, but Stew's still shut out. He doesn't seem to mind, though. He's content—for now—just to be on the river again. The water, a frigid fifty-two degrees, no longer seems cold to us. We can stand in it up to our waist for half an hour and be perfectly comfortable. Of course, it probably helps that the air temperature is approaching triple digits.

By midafternoon we're floating downstream, looking for Frog Creek, our first camping spot. It isn't far from this morning's launch, less than seven river miles. But camping this early on the first day saves us a lot of river to cover later in the trip, and Frog

Creek is a beautiful, nicely shaded little campsite, one of our favorites. There's a lot of good fishing within easy walking distance.

As we round a bend, Stewie, sitting at the bow, points ahead to the far right bank, where I can barely make out a splotch of red amid the green trees. It's the kayak, beached on the shore. Then a figure, Richard, steps from beneath the shade and out into the river, waving us into camp.

It's a good time to be coming off the water. The sun has become brutal—on a trip a few years ago, it hit 117 one day and reached highs over 110 for several days running. It's not quite that hot today, but it's close. The desert and river both fall strangely quiet this time of day; the birds, the insects, the fish, are all inactive, taking shelter from the sun. I think we're about to join them.

After beaching the boat and swapping fish lies with Richard for a couple of minutes, Stew and I unload our gear, schlepping the river bags up an incline to a natural little terrace about forty feet back from the river. Walking from the relatively cool, tree-covered canopy along the river out into the full desert heat is like walking from the air-conditioning into an oven. The temperature up there is at least twenty degrees warmer than on the river. With the heat reflecting off the light desert soil, it's enough to singe the hair off your legs.

Richard's gear is still packed on board the second raft, so he doesn't quite know what to do with himself while Stew and I unload. He pulls the three chairs off our boat and sets them up in the shallows of the river, in the shade of overhanging trees, but when he's done he just can't bring himself to sit down. He stands there, peering upstream every minute or two, waiting for us to finish.

A few minutes later, the three of us finally collapse into the chairs, beers in hand and our feet dangling in the cold water. Stewie begins to regale us with his own theory on how to catch really big fish, but he's interrupted as the third boat comes into view about a mile upriver.

We tell Richard about Marv's big fish, and about his island theory.

"Then I bet they'll be pulling over there to fish," Richard says, nodding his head upstream, where a large island sits between us and Marv's boat, about a quarter mile upriver. We sit and watch quietly for a few minutes, and sure enough, as the current draws the raft toward the island, we see Alan pulling hard on the oars toward the island's lower end.

"So now we'll see," Stewie says.

Marv has no doubt noticed that we're down here watching him. Once the raft hits the sandbar he clambers over the side and starts splashing his way downstream. There's so much current flowing through that part of the river that he doesn't worry about scaring the fish. The rush of water masks any disturbance he might make.

In the bright sunlight, his Swedish blond hair almost seems to glow with an eerie neon green. Skinny as he is, he looks like a human Q-tip from this distance.

He takes position with the water up around his thighs and makes a cross-stream cast. A few seconds later we see him pull back on his rod as a fish erupts from the water about fifty feet downstream. I hear a whoop from Alan, still sitting in their boat, watching.

Marv's pole is bent in half, and I can hear him hollering.

Damn, we're going to have to hear about this all night long.

Marv no doubt thinks he's got yet another dot in his picture of himself as the world's greatest fisherman, but me, I'm not convinced. I can take those same dots and draw a very different picture, a portrait of one lucky son of a bitch.

That's why fishing is an art, I suppose. You can come up with so many different explanations for what happened, so many different ways of connecting the dots. It's not like science, in which the dots have been located so precisely that they can be connected to draw only one possible picture.

In the days before science, our ancestors could come up with any number of explanations for why the sun rose in the east each morning and set in the west. Between those two dots, one on the right, one on the left, lay a magnificently empty canvas, to be painted however your imagination chose. In many cultures, the explanation involved a complex story about gods and goddesses and the idea of pursuit across the sky, from one horizon to the other.

That's always been the function of gods. They explained the unexplained, adding dots where otherwise there would be only a void, removing dots where otherwise the world would have seemed random chaos. The idea of gods, or later God, allowed it all to make sense, and if we still couldn't understand, that too had an explanation: It's because some things only God is capable of understanding.

God has been that blur between the lightbulbs.

As science added facts to the picture, though, the range of possible stories became more and more narrow. As it turned out, the sun is not a god, traveling across the sky in his horse-drawn chariot. It is a star, one of countless billions of stars, and the earth is a planet that orbits the star and spins on its axis. It is that spinning that creates an illusion of the sun rising each morning and setting each evening.

With few dots, or facts, truth can be multiple and flexible, connected in many ways. With many facts, truth would logically seem to drift toward the hard and singular. That expectation is what drove our intelligence agencies to respond as they have to the events of September 11—more facts, we need more facts, because then we'll understand.

But, oddly, the modern experience ought to teach us the foolishness of that approach. Because at some point in the recent past, additional facts ceased to create certainty. Instead, as facts multiplied, confusion multiplied.

There are two reasons for that, I think.

First, in many cases we're confronted by a very different form of data, the binary type consumed and generated by computers. It's a form of information and a way of thinking that is inaccessible to human beings. And as computers have grown more powerful and are given more tasks and responsibility, they make binary forms of information more powerful as well, at the expense of more human forms of information, such as story.

For a long time, I didn't appreciate how that could be a problem. The fear that computers and binary data would challenge human sovereignty seemed absurd to me, like something out of a bad science fiction movie in which rampaging computers seize control of the world. I accepted the assurance that computers were just tools under human control, and that they were a long way from challenging human intelligence.

My confidence began to wane several years ago, though, when I covered a chess match in Philadelphia between world champion Garry Kasparov and IBM's Deep Blue supercomputer.

The atmosphere surrounding the event was odd, a culture clash pitting chess nerds against computer nerds in a setting that felt reminiscent of the championship boxing matches I once covered as a journalist in Las Vegas. There was that same sense of testosterone-fueled tension, of ritualized warfare between two champions, each with its own team of seconds. The match was even billed, at least unofficially, as "Silicon vs. Meat, may the best life form win."

Kasparov, an emotional, cocky Russian, is a true showman, and before the match he promoted a romantic notion of himself as the designated champion of mankind. Until that point a computer had never beaten the world's best chess-playing human, and that, Kasparov said, was a "frontier the machine should never be allowed to cross." He saw his mission as defending "the dignity and superiority of the human race against the onslaught of the machine."

On the surface, though, it seemed that Kasparov was at a terrible disadvantage. Yes, at the time he was the undisputed world champion, a man at the peak of his game, the highest-rated player in world chess history.

But in Deep Blue, the self-described champion of mankind was pitted against a supercomputer that could accurately analyze more than 100 million chess positions each second. In the three minutes that Deep Blue usually took to decide upon a move, it could analyze up to 18 billion positions.

While that may seem absurdly excessive, it's not. At the beginning of a chess game, white and black have 20 possible moves each. If you do the math, 20×20, there are 400 possible positions on the board after just one turn. On the second move, each side might have another 24 choices, producing 230,000 possible board positions. After just three moves, there are about 150 million possible board positions, and the number continues to increase exponentially from there. It's hard to imagine, but mathematicians estimate that there are more possible positions on the chessboard than there are atoms in the universe.

But calculating power wasn't the computer's only advantage. Deep Blue could draw on a memory bank that contained every game played at the grand-master level in the previous hundred years. It had also been programmed with billions of winning endgame combinations, so that once a game came down to just a handful of pieces, the computer could not possibly make a mistake. If a late position could be won, Deep Blue was guaranteed to do so, even if it took 200 moves.

Against such a foe, I didn't see how Kasparov had a chance.

That was not, however, a concession on my part that computers were smarter than human beings. They aren't smarter than us now, they weren't then, and they probably never will be. The complexities of the real world are far vaster than those of the chessboard, and out there human powers of imagination, instinct, creativity, and learning provide a capacity that computers cannot match.

But confined to those sixty-four squares of the board, within the artificial world of chess, it was hard to see how Kasparov's natural intelligence and training could hold off the brute computing power of Deep Blue.

The games took place in a hushed, dark room inside the Philadelphia Convention Center. At one end of the room, on a slightly elevated stage, sat two chairs on either side of a small table. And on that little table sat a wooden chessboard, filled with foot soldiers and armored knights, castles and kings, arrayed in perfect military order. It was a battlefield, awaiting its generals.

The chair on the left was Kasparov's. The chair on the right faced into a computer monitor.

Sitting inside that room as the first game began, I was struck less by the chess itself—it was played at a level well beyond my appreciation—than by the body language of those involved. Kasparov would study the board intently, eyes darting, then pounce like a cat once he had decided on his move. His hands over the board were fluent and sure, moving and taking pieces with utter precision.

The Deep Blue operator would note Kasparov's move, calmly enter it into the computer via a keyboard, then sit back in his chair and wait while the computer worked.

In fact, describing the other man at the table as an "operator" seemed a stretch. Once the computer decided on the proper move, it would display its decision on the computer screen. Its human assistant would read his instructions, move the specified piece to the specified square, then sit back and await further orders.

The computer was operating the human. It was doing the thinking, issuing the orders. I've never thought the same about computers since then. The truth is, we don't operate them, at least not in the way we operate any other tool. It is at best a case of cooperation. We operate the computer; it operates us. There's a give and take with this particular machine that can make it seem almost human at times.

Deep Blue won that first game easily, just as I had expected, and after his defeat Kasparov fled the room in shame, refusing to speak to anyone. It had been a massacre, as Kasparov himself would later concede.

In subsequent days, though, things took a turn. Kasparov won the second game, then drew the third and fourth. By the fifth game, which Kasparov also won, I had come to a better understanding of how he was pulling it off. Through interviews with the champion, and by talking to the chess experts hanging around in the hall, I came to realize that top chess players approach the game as a narrative that they are trying to write.

Kasparov knew before sitting down what his opening strategy would be. He also knew what he wanted the board to look like as the game drew to an end. Most important, he knew by instinct and study what lines of play—what plotlines, so to speak—were likely to lead him to that preferred outcome, and which plotlines he had to avoid.

So rather than analyze 100 million chess positions a second—even at his best, Kasparov could analyze only three moves in that time frame—the champion simply tried to force play to follow along the lines that would lead him to victory. He tried to write the story in such a way that he would be the victor.

In the end that strategy succeeded. After winning the fifth game, Kasparov won the sixth and final game as well, taking the match with three wins, two draws, and that single, opening loss. For the time being, at least, human virtue had been successfully defended.

In one of the middle games of that match, though, I had been struck by a second insight that for me did not bode well for mankind's future at the chess table.

Months before the match, the IBM team had hired Joel Benjamin, a U.S. grand master, to help teach Deep Blue the intricacies of top-level chess. They chose Benjamin based on his reputation as a "computer killer," someone who had an uncanny knack for understanding how a computer typically played and what its weaknesses might be. In tournaments pitting man against machine, Benjamin had always done better than his rating might suggest.

At one point, I was sitting out in the convention hall with hundreds of other people, watching the game on closed-circuit television and listening as Benjamin and two other chess experts provided commentary.

All of a sudden, Benjamin let out a yelp of sorts. Deep Blue had played a very odd move, a move that neither Benjamin nor the other grand masters could understand. To them, it looked like potential disaster for the computer. But Benjamin cautioned against rushing to conclusions.

"Well, I can tell you from experience with Deep Blue, it's very often like if you're watching a basketball game and this player on your team takes a shot from thirty feet out," Benjamin said. "You go, 'No, no, no!' and then it goes in and you go, 'Yeah!'"

I was stunned. Benjamin had helped to fine-tune Deep Blue and tried to prepare it for every challenge that Kasparov might present. But once the computer was set to its task, Benjamin and his colleagues lacked the ability to comprehend what their protégé was doing or why.

As human beings, they could think of the games only in terms of narrative, a means of understanding that could take them just so far. In that particular instance, the machine had calculated so deeply into the complexities of the game that no human mind, not even those of its teachers and creators, could try to follow it.

The real-life implications of that insight are enormous. If we turn over decision-making powers to computers but are unable to judge the machine's performance, if we no longer possess the means to second-guess it and correct it, then we've lost control. We've created a system in which our connect-the-dot, story-making powers no longer apply.

Kasparov's own moment of truth came the following year, in a rematch with an even more powerful version of Deep Blue. He lost that match in a humiliating final-game meltdown, and afterward he complained that Deep Blue had made moves of such imagination and creativity that he suspected illegal intervention by the IBM team. It was hard for him to believe that decisions of such insight could have come from a computer, no matter how powerful.

"If that is the case," he said, "then they have to explain it to the rest of the world. Tell us how you accomplished it, because it's far beyond anyone's understanding. I met something I couldn't explain. People turn to religion to explain things like that."

The second threat to human comprehension of this rather bizarre world we've created is the sheer volume of information that we're expected to process. In an odd way, information overload has brought us full circle, back to the prescientific world when we had too few dots to connect, and thus were able to believe anything we wanted.

For example, what's the most thoroughly investigated crime in history? I'd suggest the assassination of President John F. Kennedy. His murder, attributed to Lee Harvey Oswald, who was himself murdered by Jack Ruby, has generated an imposing mountain of information: eyewitness testimony from people at Dealey Plaza in Dallas; forensic tests on the alleged murder weapon, on the president's body, on the Lincoln he was riding in, on the sixth-floor window at the Texas Book Depository where Oswald took aim; frame-by-frame analysis of the famous Zapruder film; extensive background investigations of Oswald, of Ruby, of those who knew Oswald and Ruby, and of those who knew those who knew Oswald and Ruby.

And over the years, all that information has been reviewed by the FBI, the CIA, the Warren Commission, congressional committees, authors, journalists, moviemakers, and countless amateur enthusiasts.

With all that information, you might think that possible explanations for the Kennedy assassination would be reduced to a universe of one. But just the opposite has happened. There is simply too much information to comprehend, and much of it is inevitably contradictory. As a result, any narrative of the events of November 22, 1963, must inevitably leave some dots unconnected and unexplained.

And those unconnected dots represent a chance for someone else preferring a different reality to draw a much different picture.

In *Libra*, his marvelous fictional account of the JFK assassination, novelist Don DeLillo imagines the plight of one Nicholas Branch, a senior CIA analyst commissioned years later to write a secret history of the event for the agency. DeLillo's version of the assassination is at once totally believable and almost certainly fanciful, but his portrait of Branch's dilemma is chilling.

An unnamed agency Curator sends Branch every bit of information the analyst requests, everything he might need to complete his narrative. But it's impossible to stop assembling data. As DeLillo describes it, the material keeps coming, more information than the analyst can handle, more than he can even organize.

"Branch sits in his glove-leather chair looking at the paper hills around him. Paper is beginning to slide out of the room and across the doorway to the house proper. The floor is covered with books and papers. The closet is stuffed with material he has yet to read. He has to wedge new books into the shelves, force them in, insert them sideways, squeeze everything together, keep everything. There is nothing in the room he can discard as irrelevant or out of date. It all matters on one level or another. This is the room of lonely facts."

These days, we all reside in the room of lonely facts. We have more facts than places to put them. They are spilling out, in need of a story to contain them. And sometimes, unfortunately, any story will do.

Before, say, the birth of Isaac Newton in 1642, the scarcity of data had required mysticism, shamanism, religion, and art to create a convincing explanation of the world around us. Newton himself devoted years to typically medieval and unscientific pursuits such as alchemy and the decoding of biblical prophecies. Those pursuits, as much as science, were products of his deep, instinctive need to understand.

Nowadays we have a lot more facts to work with. But it turns out that a world with too many dots, like a world with too few, again puts a premium on mysticism and art. It's interesting to note that by one estimate, approximately half of the 1,600 religions and denominations in the United States have been founded since just 1965.

In this chaotic culture, it's possible to find data to confirm or discredit almost any theory you care to propose. In a world in which one guess seems as good as another, it is the attractiveness of the story, not its accuracy, that determines whether it finds acceptance.

Science, once embraced as the vessel that would carry us out of dark confusion toward certainty and light, has brought us into confusion once more. It has built a world in which we know less and less about more and more, in which no real understanding seems possible and true certainty is possible only by narrowing our inquiry to a very specialized field.

Which is why the simplicity of the river is so reassuring.

Back upriver, Marv has finally landed his fish, and using two hands he briefly raises it above his head in triumph. Even from here we can tell it's a big one.

Not as big as he's going to tell us it was, but big.

Marv releases the fish to the river, then prepares to make another cast, looking for more fish. But Alan has seen enough. Across the open water we hear him yell something to Marv, then gesture him back toward the boat.

Thank God. You can tell from Marv's body language that this is not good news, but he acquiesces and starts trudging through the shallow water back to the raft.

They're coming down. In a few minutes they'll be landing here at camp, and we'll start setting up sleeping areas and getting ready to cook dinner. I pull myself out of my chair and start setting up the kitchen area. I'm tonight's chef—I'm making my specialty, shrimp jambalaya.

That evening, after dinner, after Marv has been given ample opportunity to inform us even more fully of his fishing exploits, and after Alan has had to take him down a peg by kicking his rear—again—in backgammon, we police the cooking area well. We don't want a repeat of last night's skunk invasion. Then it's time to relax and pass around the bottle.

With the sun long gone, we retire to the upper level—"the terrace," as we call it, up away from the trees that might block our view of the sky and canyon. Then we turn off the lanterns, gather the lawn chairs in a ramshackle circle again, and sit back to gaze at the stars.

Coming out of the city, it's eerie at first how dark it can be out here. You can't even see the canyon walls that you know rise all around you. The moon hasn't risen yet, so in the utter blackness you sense the canyon only as sheets of void, lines on the high horizon below which there are no stars, no nothing.

The circle of friends is quiet now, the silence broken only occasionally.

"Look, there it is," says Marv, pointing up toward the Milky Way. "The constellation of Cassiopeia, the queen, sitting in her chair. Can you see that?"

"Yeah, we know, Marv, we know."

At least once every trip, Marv has to point out Cassiopeia. It's become a running joke, but I'm not sure he realizes it yet, which makes it even better.

"Whoa! Did you see that one?" someone says, pointing to an astral glow about three feet long across the southeast sky.

"Hey, who's bogarting that whiskey? Alan? I should have known. Pass it this way."

In most years, one of us invites a newcomer along on the trip. He serves as the designated audience, our excuse for retelling the old river stories that we all want to hear and tell anyway. By now, some of those stories are about the people we used to be, when we were younger and more foolish. We've all passed forty; none of us feels immortal anymore.

With each year's retelling, though, the stories get better. The important details are highlighted; the extraneous details get dropped. Certain points are embellished—not fabricated, mind you, but . . . polished.

We don't have a newbie along on this year's trip, but that's all right. Tonight, I have a killer story to tell. I've been saving it for months, biting my tongue in telephone conversations and e-mails. It's well into the evening now, things are quieting down. It's time.

"Some of you guys know Larry, my father-in-law?"

I see a couple of heads bob up and down in the darkness. Alan knows him well. Stewart, my brother-in-law, knows him too—he married another one of Larry's daughters.

"I call Larry a real-life Zelig because of all the famous people he's known. He grew up near Hollywood in the thirties, and he was a frat brother with James Dean in community college. He directed Clint Eastwood in a play when they were both in the army. When he was a kid he played catch with William Faulkner. He says Faulkner was renting a room in his neighborhood back when the guy was writing Hollywood scripts."

"And don't forget Carol Burnett," says Stewie. "She even sent us a wedding present."

"That's right," I say. "She and Larry dated when they were in college at UCLA.

"Anyway, I thought I had heard all of Larry's Zelig stories by now, but a few months ago he told me another one. He said that when he was growing up in L.A., every summer all the boys would go to this city park to play baseball, and all the girls would go to a nearby swimming pool. And one summer, this guy named Manny showed up. Manny was a great ballplayer, and mean as a snake. When Manny told you to go play right field, you played right field.

"So years go by, Larry's just out of college and working in New York City, and he looks in the paper and sees this picture of Billy Martin, the Yankees' new second baseman. And Billy looks an awful lot like that kid Manny. So Larry gets out the baseball almanac and looks up Billy Martin. And sure enough, there it is: 'Born: Manuel Pesano.'"

"No way," says Marv.

"I know, that's what I thought too," I tell him. "But I looked it up, and that's what it says: 'Alfred Manuel Pesano.'"

"So more years go by. Larry's working at the Fort Worth newspaper, and one of his old friends from the California days comes out to visit. By now, Billy Martin is managing the Texas Rangers. So Larry uses his connections to get himself and his buddy into the clubhouse before the game.

"They walk up to Billy Martin, and Larry says, 'Manny, how you doing?'

"'Who the fuck are you, calling me Manny?' Martin says. 'Only my good friends call me Manny, and I never even met you, you asshole.'

"Larry said he thought he was about to get punched out. Martin would do that to you, you know. So Larry says, 'Manny, you may not remember, but we used to play ball together as kids, in L.A.'

"'Fuck you, man. Everybody knows I grew up in Oakland.'

"Then Martin thinks for a second. 'Oh yeah, there was that one summer my ol' lady was shacking up with some guy in L.A. Yeah, yeah, I remember that. So . . . we used to play ball together there?'

'Yeah, Manny we did. And do you remember that girl you hung out with that summer down at the pool?'

"And Billy starts to smile. 'Oh yeah, I remember her too,' he says. 'Norma, right?'

" 'That's right, Manny, Norma. Her name was Norma. Norma Baker.'

" 'So, what's your point? You married to her now or something?'

" 'Norma Jean Baker, Manny. Does that ring a bell?'

"Martin looks at him for a moment, startled. Then he starts in again. 'Fuck you, man. Fuck you. Are you telling me the first girl I ever screwed was Marilyn Monroe?'

"And Martin has Larry tossed out of the clubhouse."

The circle erupts. A couple of the guys, the ones who don't know Larry, refuse to believe the story.

"No way, man. No way that is true. That's too good."

"I know, but I think it *is* true," I insist. "Larry just got married again, to a girl he used to know back in junior high in California. And she says that Norma was one of the neighborhood kids who used to hang around."

The circle falls silent again. Richard lurches out of his chair to announce he's going to bed. It's that time, and the rest of us start to follow. A few minutes later, cozy in my sleeping bag, I stare up at the skies.

And out of the silence of the night comes a quiet voice:

"Can you imagine finding out that Marilyn Monroe was the first girl you ever laid?"

day three

I'm sitting up, my sleeping bag hunched over my shoulders against the morning coolness, my eyes fixed on the rimrock off to the west. It's early dawn, just light enough to see, but there's a tiny spot of sunshine glowing golden up on that dark canyon wall. It's the first hint of the new day.

Up there, high on the plateau, the sun must already be shining bright and hot. Dawn comes early up there. Down deep in this fissure in the earth's crust, though, early mornings are long and sweet. The sun won't climb high enough in the sky to hit us directly for a couple of hours yet, so the light is still soft and gauzy, almost feminine, blurring the sharp edges of the usually harsh desert.

The air is soft too, cool and heavy with the scent of sagebrush. The stars are gone, washed away by the dim morning light, but Venus still shines brightly in the black sky rapidly edging toward blue.

And minute by minute, as the sun rises higher, that spot of gold on the western rim grows larger; in an hour or so the entire far canyon wall will be lit up by the advancing sunshine, the advancing heat, making its way toward us.

Three of us have slept out under the stars, sharing space on the tarp spread over a sandy spot on the desert floor. The Republicans are asleep in their tents at the other end of the campsite.

For now, I'm the only one awake, maybe because my body clock is still set to East Coast time. I'd guess, just from looking around, that it's about six or so, but I'm not sure. Besides, clock time doesn't mean much here on the river.

For me, the canyon creates its own special time zone, Deschutes Standard Time. In DST, concepts such as hours and minutes are abolished. We fall asleep not long after dark and we rise with the dawn. The schedule, if you can call it that, is dictated by the sun.

We want to have the heavy work of breaking camp and reloading the rafts all but finished by the time the sun rises high enough to heat the canyon. We want to reach our next campsite by mid-afternoon so we can take shelter from the worst of the sun. We'll cook dinner in the shade of evening tonight, when the sun has again slipped behind the canyon wall, and have dinner finished by dark so we are free to watch the nightly light show before falling asleep.

We slip into that schedule easily, because even though it's not our usual cycle, it's our natural cycle. We are, after all, the product of 3 billion years of evolution here on this little blue spinning planet, and through those aeons that twenty-four-hour cycle has been imprinted on our genes and on those of all our fellow creatures, except perhaps those that live at the bottom of the ocean or deep in the soil. Day follows night, light follows dark, heat follows cold, day follows day, forever. It's our circadian rhythm, embedded in blood and bones.

So this morning, sitting in my bag watching that patch of gold creep down the far rimrock, I'm literally watching time pass, and in a most pleasant of ways.

We can see time only the way we see wind, through movement. The clock measures time by the movement of a pendulum, the spinning of a gear; an atomic clock measures it by the movement of nuclear particles. But out here it is ancient time, measured by the revolving of the planet. As the earth spins, it tips this canyon foot by foot toward the sun, and that golden glow on the far rim grows larger and larger.

Time is the world going about its business, as it did yesterday and will again tomorrow, when I am miles downstream, in another campsite, staring at another vista.

But time too is changing. We do not think of it as our ancestors did; we do not experience it in the same way.

My brother, sleeping next to me, finally starts to stir, and he opens his eyes to the world just as I look his way. I nod and smile, a wordless good morning. He nods and smiles back. Then he joins me, sitting upright in his sleeping bag, huddled against the cold. I point to the western rimrock, and he fumbles for his glasses and then looks. For a few minutes we both look, not speaking, sharing the sight and the silence.

I don't know his thoughts, but I don't have to. The moment is the same for both us.

In a little while I draw a heavy flannel shirt and a pair of jeans from my pack, dress inside the warm sleeping bag, then rise and stumble stiff-legged toward the stove. My mind has fixated on making coffee. I leave Alan there, still taking in the world and having his morning cigarette. The rest of the crew will be stirring soon. The sound of someone rattling pots, and the scent of coffee in the air, will provide a pleasant little wakeup call.

In the next couple of hours, we cook a leisurely breakfast, pack our gear, and clear the campsite. By the time we're finished, that little patch of gold on the far rimrock has spread and engulfed the world. The sun now peers straight down into the canyon, and baby, it's hot. Set your oven to four hundred degrees, wait ten minutes, and then open the oven door. That's what it feels like now, a blast of dry, windy heat.

We've all stripped down from the morning outfit of blue jeans and flannel shirts to shorts and T-shirts. And even the T-shirts won't last much longer. Stewie and Richard are riding in one raft today, Marv and Alan in the other. It's my turn in the rubber kayak.

Actually, it's not a true kayak, more like a sturdy inflatable canoe. But unlike the bargelike rafts, the kayak can skitter across the top of the river like a waterbug. And because you sit so low, right at water level, it gives you the sense of being a part of the river.

Getting into the kayak first thing in the morning is a little uncomfortable, though. It's not watertight, so when you squat down into the paddler's compartment, you put your butt in cold water. Let's just say it gives you a real intimate connection to the river.

Once the packing's done we all shove off, and in just a few minutes I've scooted so far ahead that the boats are no longer even in sight behind me. It's as though I've got the river to myself.

The early part of today's ride will be a gentle drift, punctuated by a few minor class 2 rapids. Then there's one major stretch of white water to handle, Whitehorse, before we pull off to camp for the night.

We have traveled the river for so many years now that much of the passing scenery has become a setting for various stories, layer upon layer of them, sights that stir memories.

A few years back, on that steep rocky face to the right, my friend Kent lost his balance trying to climb down to a fishing spot. He tumbled head over heels, about fifteen feet down the cliff, landing backward on his head in a tangle of briar. I was about twenty feet away when he fell, and had to crash through the briar bushes to get to him. When I finally spotted him, he lay in a heap on the rocks, limbs splayed. He was silent, he wasn't moving, and from where I stood, I could see a flow of blood running from the back of his head across his face.

That scared me to death, but from Kent's perspective the experience was even more frightening. He told us later that when he first regained consciousness, he could hear me crashing through the briar bush, yelling for him. He tried to respond, to move, but his body wouldn't obey. For a few seconds—it seemed like forever to him, but it could have been only a few seconds—he thought he had been paralyzed.

In the end, Kent came out of the fall with a nasty little scalp wound on the back of his head. We cleaned it and dressed it from our rudimentary first-aid kit, and kept him confined to the boat or campsite for a day, just in case he had suffered a concussion.

We now travel with an upgraded first-aid kit, and Kent became legendary in the annals of the Deschutes. In fact, he has an official title. Whenever we reminisce about the year that he came on the river, we refer to him as Kent, the River Rat Who Shook Off Paralysis.

Right over there, in a back eddy along another sheer rock face, is the Whorehouse. I made my annual visit there just last night, as the jambalaya simmered, and once again did very well. It's a great little fishing spot, and every time I'm there I think of another friend, Steve.

He was forty-eight the year he made the trip, and had never been fishing or camping in his life. In preparing for the trip, I gave him a list of the equipment he would need, and he went to the sporting goods store and bought it all, brand-new and top of the line. In his first day on the river, he looked like one of those eastern dudes in an old-fashioned Western, spanking new and clean.

Richard was so jealous.

Steve and I fished hard together on his first day on the river, trying to hook him up with a fish. I would point him to the best spots, make sure he was rigged up correctly, but by evening he hadn't caught a thing and was getting discouraged.

"C'mon," I told him at camp. "We're hiking to a special place and get you a fish. You can't sit around tonight with no fish story to tell."

"No, I'm beat. You go ahead."

"Uh-uh. You have to come. I guarantee you'll catch fish."

He still wasn't buying it, so I struggled to come up with a way to explain it better.

"This spot's like a whorehouse," I finally said. "Everybody's guaranteed to get lucky."

So he came along, he caught four nice fish in about twenty minutes, and he returned to camp a proud and smiling man. That spot has been dubbed the Whorehouse ever since. No Tijuana brothel ever made a virgin happier.

As I swing around the bend, I see Trout Creek ahead, the campground where we stayed two nights earlier. After just a day of isolation on the river, the sight of so many people—there must be fifteen or twenty at least—is jarring. The cars and boat trailers scattered at the campsites look as out of place now as hay wagons in downtown Manhattan. I paddle hard, to put it behind me as quickly as possible.

Just past the campground, off to the right, a railroad line swings down off the plateau along the Trout Creek riverbed, then heads north right alongside the Deschutes, on a bed carved out of the canyon more than a century ago. Two or three freights make their way up the Deschutes each day, carrying grain and lumber out of the Columbia Valley. They climb out of the canyon here at Trout Creek, grind their way up to the high plateau, and then highball it south toward California.

It's funny. You can be floating through a picturesque, deceptively pristine part of the canyon and then hear the rumble of a freight chugging up the incline. And somehow it doesn't seem out of place. The Deschutes isn't true wilderness. But with ranches and abandoned outbuildings along the river, not to mention the railroad, the landscape has a nineteenth-century, Western feel to it.

Now, just past some small, splashy rapids where Trout Creek empties into it, the Deschutes turns slow and wide, suiting my mood perfectly. With two hard strokes of the paddle I put the kayak into a lazy spin, then lie back and close my eyes.

We're such visual creatures, especially in this modern media age, that we seldom give our other senses a chance to show us what they can do, what information and sensations they can bring us if we will only let them dominate us.

I hear the flowing water, and feel its gentle rocking beneath me even as I spin. The clean river scent is sweet in my nostrils. The mid-morning sun is behind me, upstream, and as I spin clockwise in the water I feel its intense warmth first on my right cheek, then full face, then on my left cheek, then finally on my back. I'm a one-man planet, slowly spinning, turning from light to shadow and back again, and with each rotation the current carries me a little farther downstream.

I open my eyes to make sure there are no obstacles ahead, give it another couple of strokes with the paddle, and return to my reverie.

There's nowhere I have to be, no one to meet, no obligations. Out here, time is not artificial and manufactured, hours ground into minutes, minutes ground into seconds. It is not parceled out to me in doses measured by the ticking of the clock, as if time were so much chicken feed doled out to hungry chickens.

Here, time is a flow, like the river flows, like thoughts flow, in a stream of consciousness. Sometimes it moves swiftly, at other times slowly. An hour can seem like a day, or like just a few minutes. And like the river, but unlike thought, time always moves in one direction.

I like the sense of time sweeping us downstream, allowing us to look back but never to go back, the flow of the river too strong to buck. I like the fact that struggle against the current is hopeless, but we struggle anyway.

Back home, I find myself surrounded by watches and clocks. I have clocks on my computer, my car dashboard, my stove, my microwave, my cable TV box, VCR, radio, telephone, fax machine, cell phone, all insisting that I know what time it is.

The clock turns time into a commodity. It breaks the flow into prepackaged units that can be bartered away for money, as if time were so much flour or beef. An hour of a human life carries a price tag: ten dollars an hour, five dollars an hour, two hundred dollars an hour. The value of your time has become a measure—for a lot of people the most important measure—of your worth as a human being. Even the government now thinks of its citizens that way. In wrongful-death suits, the courts dispense compensation to families based on how much money the victim had been earning and could be expected to earn if life had not been cut short.

Since time is truly money, we constantly look for ways to conserve it, to use it more efficiently. We try to whittle a few minutes here, a few minutes there from every task. Saving time is good; wasting time is evil. We talk of stealing time or borrowed time, and are cautioned to invest our time wisely; time can be well spent or misspent, but it is spent any way you look at it.

Today, we rely more heavily on measured time than any society in history. The clock has literally synchronized modern life, giving it a precise, exact tempo, just as a conductor gives a symphony its direction and rhythm.

Think about your daily routine:

"I told him we'd meet him at three."

"Give me another thirty minutes; I'll have it on your desk."

"We'd better be going; our reservation's at seven."

"Can you set the alarm for six? I've got an early meeting."

Without the clock, the finely tuned gears of modern life would begin to clash, and then lurch, and then grind to a noisy halt, the symphony reduced to cacophony.

The analog clock, with its hour and minute hands spinning around the clock face, at least preserves the sense of time as a natural, organic cycle. Once around with the second hand constitutes a minute; one revolution of the minute hand marks an hour; and two revolutions of the hour hand completes a day.

But in our electronic economy, we increasingly measure time by the digital clock, a clock in which the symbolic link to time as either a flow or a cycle is lost entirely. With the digital clock—the computer's clock—time is reduced to a succession of numbered units, and each unit pinpoints an exact spot in time just as surely as longitude and latitude pinpoint a spot on the globe.

The nature of time has been transformed in another way as well. In the modern economy we move more quickly, do more things in less time, do more things at the same time, and schedule ourselves in ever tighter increments. Time, after all, is a finite resource, and to make the most of it we human beings are imitating our computers by multitasking.

These constant claims on our attention, together with the distributed, chaotic nature of our lifestyles, have disrupted our narrative of self. Life, which like time and work once flowed freely and unencumbered, the next event building on the last, no longer flows at all. The way we live, one activity or responsibility or thought too often has no discernible relationship to the next task that demands our attention.

Life is instead lived as a series of rushed and disconnected moments, each happening to follow the other in sequence but otherwise unrelated to one another. The narrative string has been cut. Connecting the dots has become impossible.

I think that's why hobbies, sports, and other diversions have become increasingly precious to so many people: They allow us to "lose ourselves" in something, which is actually an odd way to describe what happens.

In my experience, we do not lose ourselves in large chunks of unfragmented time; rather, we find ourselves. We pull together the various pieces of our fragmented self and focus them again on a single purpose, a single goal, a single activity. We may work very hard at such pursuits—in fact, one of the requirements of a hobby or sport is that it absorb all of our concentration and focus. But in the end we come away refreshed and satisfied, recentered and renewed.

The sense of calm and peace that we get from total immersion is what psychologist Mihaly Csikszentmihalyi calls "the flow." He defines it as "a state in which action follows action according to an internal logic which seems to need no conscious intervention on our part. . . . We experience it as a unified flowing from one moment to the next, in which we feel in control of our actions, and in which there is little distinction between past, present and future."

Csikszentmihalyi reserves "flow" to describe those relatively rare moments when an athlete is "in the zone," or when a person is so thoroughly immersed in a task that he is operating at a peak of creativity and productivity. I would borrow his term but define it more broadly, to apply to any task that attracts and holds our attention for an extended period of time, and that leaves us feeling rejuvenated and less harried.

Unfortunately, even by that broader definition of "flow," it is an increasingly rare experience. By channel-surfing through our own lives, never staying on any task long enough to pick up the story line, never experiencing that flow, we have lost track of our personal plot and narrative. We have trouble connecting the dots that make up our own lives.

Increasingly, that sense of human time has given way to computer time, and a computer has no use for the charms of narrative. We who need it must defend it. We must consciously reassert it, make sure that we make space for it in our daily lives.

The change began, I think, with the Industrial Revolution. Imagine yourself as a preindustrial cobbler. You handle every part of the making of a pair of shoes, from preparing the leather to cutting the pieces to sewing the leather together. It isn't very efficient, but there's an undeniable psychic pleasure in seeing a task through from beginning to completion. When you finish a shoe, you can hold it in your hand and know it is your doing. You made that thing.

Now consider that same process performed in a factory. Each person performs a single piece of the task—the sewing of the tongue, the cutting of the sole—over and over again. The process is far more efficient, and because of that efficiency the cost of the final product is lower, allowing many more people to afford shoes. On the whole, it is undeniably a better economic system. But there's no "flow" to work performed that way.

Take that model and compare it to your daily life. How often are you the cobbler, seeing a single task through to a satisfying completion? Or have you become more like a one-person factory, many different parts of yourself performing many different tasks, each of those selves only vaguely aware of contributing some piece to the final product that is rumored to be your life?

Technology will rob us of the stillness we need. If permitted, it will intrude on us, break our time and attention into little pieces. It disrupts our story line.

If we let it.

We need to give ourselves time that flows like the river flows, time in which one thought can drift easily and logically into the next and then the next, eventually carrying your mind to places and connections not otherwise accessible to us in the jumble and chaos of modern life.

There are no roads to such places, no shortcuts. Roads and shortcuts require that you know your destination, and in this case if you know where your head is going, you're not having any fun at all.

It took me awhile to learn that, even here on the river. In the first few years we came out here, we were a lot more aggressive in our fishing. We brought the competitive spirit of the outside world here into the canyon, as you might expect when guys gather for such a trip. We would keep close count of how many fish we caught each day, carefully eyeing each other's progress to ensure no "fish stories" were being told. The man who caught the most fish at the end of the trip was awarded custody of a fishing reel, spray-painted gold and mounted on a cheap wooden plaque.

But Alan and Stewart, each contributing in a very different way, eventually broke us of that habit.

Alan is to fishing on the Deschutes what Brad Pitt is to women in a Hollywood bar. He's always going to catch more than you. Year after year he won the trophy, and after a while it became clear to the rest of us that he was simply a better and more determined fisherman.

But the competition really started falling apart when Stewart started coming on the trips.

I love Stewart. He is a good man. But Stewart is—how shall I say this?—a man of more exuberance than discipline.

He's also a man who—again, how can I put this politely?—he has a very "fluid" sense of numbers. Like the rest of us, he catches a lot of fish each day, but in his mind "a lot" could be expressed by any one of several numbers. Eight was certainly a lot, but so was twelve or fifteen. Stewart apparently couldn't see why it mattered if he called the day's catch "fifteen" instead of "eight." So he often chose fifteen.

That approach inspired a lot of campground grumbling, some of it to Stewart's face. But he is not a man easily dissuaded from his worldview, and in time, the rest of us came to see wisdom in his ways. We were all catching a lot of fish, so who cared if, every year, Alan caught a few more than we did? What did it matter, eight, twelve, or fifteen? Stewie exposed the whole idea of competing by fish count as ridiculous.

The funny thing is, Stewart's the entrepreneur among us. Through a lot of hard work and lean times, he and his wife, Susie, have built a small publishing business into a thriving, profitable enterprise.

And I suspect that their success can be explained in part by Stewart's sense that the realities of the world are not set in stone, but rather can be rearranged to his liking.

But I sure would hate to be his accountant.

It's been a while since I've seen anybody else from our party. While I've been floating—"flowing," if you will—they've probably been beached somewhere back upriver, catching the first fish of the day. So I paddle over and float along the bank, looking for a place to beach the kayak.

Finally I see a promising spot, a place where the river swirls into a sweet little back eddy. You catch some nice fish in places like that. The big boys just sit down there, letting the swirling river bring dinner to them.

In the big, lumbering raft I wouldn't be able to reach that spot; the river current would just wash me past it. But the kayak is much more maneuverable.

Even with a kayak, though, a landing like this requires a delicate touch. You want to beach yourself quietly enough that you don't spook any fish who might be hanging around. But you also need to be noisy enough to announce your presence to any rattlesnakes that might be lurking.

A few years ago, when I was landing in a spot like this, I reached out from the kayak to grab a bush to steady myself in the current. And just as I extended my hand, I noticed a rattler coiled at the base of the bush, warming itself in the sun. I pulled my hand back and glided on by, a little rattled my ownself. It had been a damn fine fishing spot, but . . .

This time there are no rattlers, or at least none that I could see. I pull the kayak ashore, grab my fishing rod, and wade out into the river, bracing myself against the current. The water doesn't feel anywhere near as cold as it did yesterday.

I pull the treble hook free from the cork handle of the fishing rod, reach back behind me, and then flick the lure out into the river, letting the current swing it back toward the bank, where the fish lie.

And there it is. First cast again. The rod starts to vibrate hard in my hand, and then comes a series of strong tugs before the fish darts away, pulling line off my reel in its dash for safety.

An hour or so later, I've caught and released three nice rainbows. The second hooked up just as Marv and Alan floated by, an excellent accident of timing. You always want to have a fish on your line when somebody else floats by. It really racks up the style points. They even dropped off a cold beer, and I'm sitting here drinking it, waiting for Stew and Richard Gear to come up behind me. Their cooler holds our lunch supplies, and I'm ready for a sandwich. Besides, Whitehorse is still ahead, and I'm not interested in bouncing through a major rapid in this flimsy little kayak. I want to hitch a ride in the big boat.

The sun's hot, and I'm at peace, lying in the high grass along the bank, keeping an eye on the river and halfheartedly trying not to fall asleep. If I don't catch Stew as he floats by, they'll probably go right on downstream without even noticing me here, hidden in the reeds along the bank.

In his book *Coming Up for Air,* written in 1939, George Orwell writes as touching a paean to moments such as this as I've ever read. It turns out that as a boy in England he loved to fish. He writes of catching dace and chub and gudgeon, whatever the hell those are. Like any real fisherman, he admits, "My best fishing memory is about some fish that I never caught."

"I've still got, I've always had, that peculiar feeling for fishing," he writes. "You'll think it damned silly, no doubt, but I've actually half a wish to go fishing even now, when I'm fat and forty-five and got two kids and a house in the suburbs. . . .

"As soon as you think of fishing you think of things that don't belong to the modern world. The very idea of sitting all day under a willow tree beside a quiet pool—and being able to find a quiet pool to sit beside—belongs to the time before the war, before the radio, before aeroplanes, before Hitler."

Slowly, the pleasure—the luxury—of a nap in the tall grass becomes too much to resist. I give in. I lie back, tilt my baseball cap down over my face, and drift gently into a light sleep. I am soon unconscious, yet somehow aware through it all of the immense sensuous pleasure of the experience.

It's as if I'm dreaming, and in the dream I'm napping by the side of a wild and beautiful river, hot sun on my body, listening to the sound of the water flowing past me, without me for a while. The sense of control, of maintaining consciousness even in the midst of sleep, is so strong that after a while, I feel myself slowly deciding to wake up, to end the dream. And so I do.

But that sense of control was an illusion. I realize that I have no idea how long I was out. It could have been five minutes or forty-five. I sit up and look upstream . . . no sign of that big blue raft. It's possible that they're still upstream, but I doubt it. They probably floated by while I slept, which means that I have some ground to make up.

Still half giddy from my nap, I stow my fishing gear and empty beer can in the kayak, preparing to move on. Even the feel of cold, wet water on my butt as I sit in the kayak isn't enough to break the spell.

But then, as I paddle out into the river and let the current sweep me up, I remember. Somewhere up ahead, between me and tonight's campsite, lies Whitehorse, the most dangerous rapid on this section of the river. I've now put myself in the position of having to do Whitehorse in an inflatable kayak, hardly the most stable craft on the river, without a raft in sight to bail me out if I get in trouble.

If it were any other rapid, I might be able to beach the kayak and carry it downstream on my shoulders, below the white water. But

Whitehorse is about two miles long, far too long to portage around.

It's not a total disaster. I've thought often about trying White-horse this way, just for the hell of it, but I've always chickened out. Now the decision has been made for me.

A few years ago, Marv made the same trip down Whitehorse in a kayak, but that was even more of an accident than my predicament. It's so easy to get lost out here. So many bends of the river look like so many others. And the sun doesn't help any. It doesn't make you addled, but it does bake the attention out of you, broiling you into a pleasant, brainless stupor. For whatever reason, Marv lost track of where he was on the river and found himself staring down the throat of Whitehorse before he realized it. He made it through, but not without fearing for his life.

Over the next couple of miles I paddle quickly, just in case I can catch up to Stew and Richard. I'm also keeping a close eye on the right bank for—damn, there it is—a sheer lava cliff, covered in lime green lichen. It's the warning sign that Whitehorse is just ahead.

I pull over to the bank, beach the kayak, and hike downstream about a quarter mile, until I'm high on a cliff looking down at the head of the rapids. As I look downstream, there are no other boats in sight.

In a raft I probably wouldn't bother to scout the run; the big inflatables are much more forgiving of a mistake, and I've run it many times. But a rubber kayak tips easily, and if you make a mistake as simple as taking the wrong angle, you're out of the boat, in the drink, swimming for your life, with your fishing gear sacrificed to the river gods.

Right now, it looks deceptively easy. You can see how swiftly the water's moving, but from up here on the cliff, the height flattens the waves. You really can't appreciate their power unless you're down there, in their grip.

Whitehorse is essentially a boulder field, which means you need to pick your line through it like a running back in an open field picks his way through tacklers. The best entry point for the run is about thirty feet off the right bank. Once you're past the initial boulders—Oh Shit Rock is the most infamous—you need to move quickly off to the left, ride through the series of ten-foot standing waves, then swing quickly back to the right. If you make those maneuvers successfully, the rest of the run is fairly easy.

On the hike back, I rehearse the run in my head . . . start on the right, go left, go right. As long as I'm in the kayak, remembering that sequence won't be all that important, because I can maneuver quickly. But if I end up in the water I become a lot less mobile, and I need to have that plan in my head so I won't panic.

Back at the kayak, I tighten my life jacket, lash my fishing gear to the boat, and stash my sunglasses in my fanny pack. Then I shove off into the river. The current, much stronger now, grabs the kayak almost immediately. As I come swinging to the right around the bend, Whitehorse opens up in front of me, and I can hear its roar. I get the sinking feeling that I may have bitten off more than I can chew.

Sitting in a raft, your head is about five feet above the water, and you can see a long way downstream, so you know what's coming. In the kayak, I'm right at water level, and the waves and rocks look enormous. In fact, everything looks different from down here. I can't recognize the clear line I had picked out up on the cliff. And in a few seconds I won't have time to think.

Okay, thirty feet off the right bank, you know that much. Is this thirty feet? If I misjudge five feet to the right or left, I'm in trouble. There's the chute, now cheat a little bit to the left, that's where I want to be. . . .

Too far left. Oh shit.

I hit the rock head-on and hear the kayak crumpling around me. It's a terrible sound. Then—I have no concept of it happening, time skips forward a few seconds—I suddenly find myself underwater, tumbling in the froth, trying desperately to get back to the surface but uncertain even where "up" is. I open my eyes, but all I see is white. And I'm being tumbled like a sock in a washing machine.

Finally I break the surface, brought up by the buoyancy of the life vest. I grab a breath, pivot to look downstream—another rock coming fast. I put myself in the proper sitting position, legs downriver to absorb the impact. My feet hit the rock, the river at my back crushes me forward, my knees buckle—ooomph, I'm slammed into the rock, the life vest acting like a flak jacket, protecting my ribs from the impact.

For a terrifying moment I'm pinned to the rock by the crush of water, unable to move, but I twist my body, trying to create a new angle. The river washes me free just as the kayak floats by, unoccupied, like a ghost ship. I grab for it, and as I clutch rubber, relief and gratitude surge through my body. A few seconds later I spot the paddle floating nearby. I snatch it and stow it on board.

Okay, I'm still being washed downstream like a piece of flotsam, but things are looking better. As the panic subsides I notice for the first time how damn cold the water is. And right at the moment, getting back into the kayak isn't possible. I've got some immediate maneuvering to do.

I side-kick left, trying to set up position for the standing waves. Oh boy. Up and down, up and down, while the river tries to rip the kayak from my grasp. High on the crest of the last wave I look downstream, plotting my course, then start to kick hard to the right again, back into position.

It's still too rough to try climbing back into the kayak. Besides, I feel a sudden need for firm earth beneath my feet. I start kicking—hard—toward the right shore. Ouch! My leg smacks a rock hidden underwater, right on the thigh. That's really going to hurt later. *Oww!* Another one, on my left shin. I should still have my feet pointed downstream, but I'm trying to feel something solid, solid, solid. . . .

There.

Solid.

My feet touch ground, and I stumble through the water toward a shallow riffle on the right, pulling the kayak behind me. I yank the boat up onto the rocks and then stand there, my chest heaving and my legs quivering uncontrollably beneath me.

I bend at the waist, trying to catch a breath, and as I look down, hands on my shaking knees, I see a ribbon of red running down my left shin, bleeding into my white sock. And I find myself smiling.

What a fucking rush.

Once I catch my breath I collapse into the kayak, the rubber already dry and warm in the desert heat. It takes a while for my head to clear of images of white water and panic, even absolute fear.

The images follow no story line, no sequence; they just rush at me, and I can't stop them. I can't piece them back together, can't decide what happened when. Certain moments are crystal clear; others are just blurs. Some seem to have occurred in excruciatingly slow motion, others at a speed too fast to register.

I lie there for a while, until my legs steady, the adrenaline washes through my system, and I can think straight. It probably takes fifteen minutes, maybe half an hour before I'm looking around at the scenery again. And then, having been tossed from the horse, it's time to mount up again, to get back in the kayak and get downstream.

We always camp just at the end of Whitehorse, about another mile downstream, and the white water is pretty straightforward between here and there. But when the adrenaline left, it took my cockiness with it. I'm more than a little apprehensive settling back into that kayak for the rest of the trip.

Tonight, my little misadventure is the talk of the camp. Unbeknownst to me, the guys had figured out that something had gone wrong for me upstream.

"We were sitting here in the shade waiting for you," Alan tells me. "Then Stewie pointed out to the river and said, 'Hey, isn't that your brother's Red Sox hat floating by out there?' That was kind of a clue."

All in all, though, I came out all right. The gash on my shin probably could use a few stitches, but the cut is clean and will heal fine. In time it will leave a dark, bruiselike scar. My right thigh is banged up pretty badly. The kayak is no worse for wear, and unlike its owner, my fishing gear somehow stayed on board, so no loss there either.

Hey, I even got my hat back.

Tonight, we're all pretty quiet. We're beat by a full day on the river, me especially. I'm sucking down aspirin from the first-aid kit, trying to fend off the soreness I know is going to hit after the day's adventure and a night of sleeping on the hard ground.

Marv tries to generate some enthusiasm for backgammon. He especially wants a piece of Alan, for revenge, but tonight he gets no takers.

Tomorrow we're just going to hang out all day, so we're all settling in, putting some extra touches to the campsite that we wouldn't bother with if we were going to hit the river again tomorrow. Stewart has put up his tent, joining the Republicans for the next couple of nights and leaving Alan and me out on the tarp.

The campsite—Big Bend, we call it—sits on the inside edge of a sharp turn of the river, where the water comes roaring straight out of Whitehorse and then takes a sixty-degree turn to the right. This evening, Richard takes a beautiful photograph of the scene from a hillside a few hundred feet away.

In the photo, the sun has almost dipped over the western rim, and in the foreground the evening shadows have fallen. The day is coming to a close. The tents are up, the chairs are in position facing the river, and a few of us are standing around talking, the river at our backs. We're all wearing long pants, as the cool has already fallen.

But off in the background, the evening sun still lights up the far hillside in a glorious white-silver brilliance.

It's a beautiful moment; but even though I'm certain I was present to see it, I don't have any memory of it. It must have seemed to me like just another pleasant evening on the river.

Through that photograph, though, that moment has been snatched out of the flow of time and frozen for me, like a butterfly caught and pinned to a display board. Now I can look at it, hold it in my hand, and appreciate how beautiful it was. One of the marvels of the human mind is its ability to free us from the confines of the human body. The mind can take us places the body cannot, even upstream, against the flow of time, to moments long since gone.

day four

Oh baby. I am hurting.

I mean everything aches: My back. My ribs, shoulders . . . legs.

My legs are hamburger. My left shin has a nice gash. My right thigh aches down to the bone.

I should still be sleeping. I would be, except it hurts too damn much. I lie in my sleeping bag, looking around, trying to summon enough courage to do something.

It looks to be early morning, predawn, and the sky is a deep royal blue, with a few stars still bright enough to be seen. Off to the east, behind us, a light tinge is beginning to creep over the canyon wall.

So, first things first: Where did I leave that aspirin bottle?

Oh yeah, in my shaving kit, which is right . . . over there. I unzip my sleeping bag and roll awkwardly, gingerly, out onto the tarp. I get to my feet and stumble stiff-legged toward the aspirin. I'm in my underwear, and I'm cold, and in the dim light I'm trying to pick my way across the desert floor in my bare feet. It's like tiptoeing blind across a minefield.

Man, if anyone were awake to see me like this, he'd be howling.

Sure hope there are no snakes or scorpions out here.

There's the aspirin bottle. Thank God. Now, how many should I take? Shake out one, two . . . three?

Three. Definitely three. I shiver in the cold, trying to hurry so I can scurry back into the warm bag.

Someone stirs in one of the tents. Probably awakened by the rattle of aspirin as I try to get this last damn . . . Got it. Twist the lid back on, then close my fist tight around the pills.

Okay, step two: I need Gatorade, to wash 'em down. I scan the camp. Right there, an unopened bottle by my backpack.

Twist open the bottle, throw back the dry aspirin, take a mouthful of Gatorade. Another swallow, then another. Boy that tastes good. Cuts the morning crud.

Remedicated, I stumble back to the tarp, brush the dirt off my feet, then burrow back down into the sleeping bag, covering my head against the morning chill and the lightening sky, hoping I'll feel better if I can get back to sleep and wake up a couple of hours from now.

Sometime later I wake up in a full sweat. Even with my head buried deep inside the darkness of my bag, I can tell that the sun has come up over the canyon rim and is now shining at full strength on our campsite. It's turned my bag into a sauna.

I poke my head out and take a welcome gulp of fresh air. Damn it's bright out there.

"Morning, Jay," someone says, standing right over me. I look up . . . my eyes are still trying to adjust to the light, and all I can see is a silhouette against the bright sky. But even in silhouette, Stew cuts a distinctive figure.

"I saw you limping around early this morning. You looked pretty bad," he says. "You all right?"

I don't respond. . . . I'd like to know the answer myself. So I lie there for a moment, taking stock of my various body parts.

"Feeling better than I was, anyway," I finally answer. "Is there coffee yet?"

"Yeah. Want me to bring you some?"

"No thanks. I need to get up and out of the sun anyway."

Stewie nods, and meanders off toward the river, where we've set up the chairs and the cooking area. I hear the murmur of voices down there, mingling with the murmur of the river.

I tug on a pair of shorts and a fresh T-shirt, and a few minutes later I'm making my way down the hill to the kitchen area. I'm still not the epitome of style and grace, but I do feel better. As I reach the circle of chairs I'm greeted with a smattering of smart-ass applause.

Richard jumps up and starts to pull my chair into place for me.

"No thanks, I think I need to stand, walk around and get loose. If I sit I'll never get up again."

"You all right, bro?" Alan asks, pointing at my right leg. "Whoa. It left a mark."

I look down at my thigh. I hadn't yet seen it in full daylight. There, just above the knee, is a deep dark splotch of blue and purple and red, about as big as my fist, with what looks to be a little yellow and even green thrown in as well.

"Well, that's impressive," I say, recalling in my mind the particular rock that did it to me. A little lower and it would've smashed me right on the kneecap, maybe doing some real damage. "River beat the shit out of me, didn't it?"

"River did," Alan concurs.

Richard, over at the stove, pours a cup of coffee from the pot and silently hands it to me. I nod in gratitude and wrap my hands around the hot cup. I take a sip. It tastes great, black and strong. Then Richard starts banging on the side of the tin stove with a spatula, like a maestro striking the podium with a baton to get his orchestra's attention.

All conversation ceases.

"My name is Rich-ard," he says, using the French pronunciation, "and I will be your chef zis fine morning. Today, I will be preparing for you a main course of scrambled eggs avec fromage and fresh-sliced toe-mah-toes, with a side of German bratwurst, steamed slowly in our finest Budweiser. And oh yes, hash browns and onions left over from those potatoes we boiled last night."

Marv leans over to me.

"Aren't you glad we made reservations? I hear that if you don't call at least two weeks ahead, you can never get in this place."

I glance at Richard. He's eating this up.

Armed with his shopping list, Stewie jumps up and starts rummaging through the two large food coolers, digging out the requested items. It's the perfect job for him. Thanks to his constant foraging, Stewie has memorized the exact location of every food item that we have with us. He's a human food Google. Tell him what you want, he'll find it.

Marv gets up to refill his coffee cup, then heads off to his tent to fetch a fresh pack of cigarettes.

Alan watches him leave.

"You should have seen him yesterday, when your hat floated by," Alan says quietly.

"Who? You mean Marv?"

"Yeah. We were all sitting here, laughing at you, wondering what had happened. Stew walked out in the water to get your hat, but Marv, man, he jumped up, grabbed his first-aid kit and some ropes out of our raft, and just took off like he was on a nine-one-one call, rushing upstream to save your ass."

"Meanwhile, the rest of you guys just sat here?"

"Shit yeah, we were comfortable. Besides, it was hot out there."

I look at him, waiting.

"Okay, so yeah, we did try to follow him, but you know, that guy can move! Must be all that basketball. He left us in the dust. I bet he was about a half mile upstream before we saw him stop and start walking back down our way. I guess he finally saw you coming down in the kayak and knew you were all right."

I laugh at the image of Marv bounding up the river like that, but the story makes me feel good. These guys are important to me. We're important to each other.

Some of us—Marv and me, and certainly Alan and me—had strong connections before we ever started making these river trips. If you think of the five of us as interconnected like a spiderweb, those two relationships would be the foundation strands, the threads that connect the river crew to something solid in the outside world.

Other strands of the web have been woven out here, during our time on the river. Stew's my brother-in-law, and until we started taking this trip, he and Alan knew each other only slightly. Neither of them had ever met Marv and Richard. Now we've all become good friends. No big surprise, I guess. Add up all the days over all the years, and we've spent a couple of months or more together out here.

During the rest of the year, we're spread to the four winds. We e-mail each other several times a week, and talk on the phone fairly often as well, to share a laugh or a bit of family news. It lets us stay in touch, which is good.

But it's nothing like being out here. "Your male-bonding trip," my wife calls it, and she's right. It's embarrassing to admit how much of our phone conversations during the rest of the year are spent either laughing about something that happened on the river, or looking ahead to the trip coming up.

People talk a lot about the social possibilities raised by new technology: e-mail friendships, chat rooms, the whole range of connections made possible by electronic communication. To some degree it's true. The Internet allows us to role-play, or find a community that shares almost any aspect of our nature or interest, from bird-watching to chess to ska. It has become a new, multichanneled means of exploring our new, multichanneled beings. If you listen to the techno-enthusiasts, even time and distance have been eliminated as restraints on human sociality. Everyone in the world—or everybody with Internet access—is potentially my best friend.

I don't buy it. Trying to eliminate time as a constraint on friendship, or on any human relationship . . . that's like trying to eliminate money as a constraint on the economy. Time is our most precious resource. It is never replenished, always diminishing. We can never go back upstream. So true friendships are built on the mutual willingness to spend that time together. There's no substitute, technological or otherwise, for that.

Claims that technologies can eliminate space or distance as restraints are just as suspect. John Podesta, chief of staff in the Clinton administration, tells a story about a company that was trying to sell the White House on its top-of-the-line videoconferencing system for the Situation Room, the command center where officials gather in times of crisis. A company executive bragged to Podesta that with a broadband connection, his product's video picture and sounds were so sharp and lifelike that it would seem as though the other person were right there in the room, even though he might be thousands of miles away.

"I told him no, we weren't interested, but he was really insistent," Podesta recalled. "He kept telling me how great it was. Finally, I think he got a little frustrated and asked what my objection was. So I told him: 'When you're working in a crisis situation with someone, when you're counting on them under pressure, you want to be shoulder to shoulder with him. You want to be able to smell the other guy's sweat.'"

(Since then I've read that the Situation Room, under "new management," has been equipped with full videoconferencing capability. Time marches on; the river flows.)

If the Internet does free us from certain constraints, they include the constraints of being honest in our social relationships, of being polite and kind so that we might be treated with equal kindness in return. In the virtual world, there are rarely consequences for how we behave, and it shows in the number of mean and vicious sons of bitches you encounter.

A lot of people have commented on the increasing rudeness of the modern world, a complaint that every generation seems to make about its successors. To the degree that that's true about our own time, I'd have to believe that some of that meanness has migrated out of the virtual world into the real.

Here on the river, you can't lie, except about fishing. You are who you are, and you'd better be comfortable with that. If things start going bad with your colleagues, as they have from time to time among us, you can't just change chat rooms. You have to work it out. The patron saint of river rafting, one Huckleberry Finn, said it best:

"What you want, above all things on a raft, is for everybody to be satisfied, and feel right and kind towards the others."

Amen, Brother Huck.

Yes, I suppose that by tonight, after we've all had a few beers, Richard could get up and tell us that he is really a seventeen-year-old lesbian from Japan. But I don't believe he would fool many of us.

I don't mean all this as a condemnation of the Internet. I use it, I enjoy it, I'm entertained by it, and as a journalist I would never want to do without it. My job is easier, and I can do it far better, because I have the Internet as a resource.

But those who champion the Web as a revolutionary tool for satisfying human social needs—I'm sorry, it just doesn't come close.

To the contrary, the Web's ability to mimic true social interaction is its greatest danger. Virtual is a simulation of the real, but as Podesta pointed out, it is not real. No speaker system can reproduce precisely the sound of the river gurgling in the background right now; no computer or TV screen can re-create this 360-degree, ground-to-sky view; certainly, no artificial system can even begin to approximate the feel of this brilliant sunshine, the breath of wind on my skin at the moment.

To the degree that we experience life and each other mediated through electronic means, we cheat ourselves. It is a poor substitute for the real thing.

For example, the word "smile" is understood to be a mere representation of a smile, a symbol that evokes the image of a smile in the reader's mind. It is not intended to function as the smile itself.

But in cyberlingo, :>) is more than a word. In the cyberworld it functions not as a symbol but as a smile itself. Yet it is a sad, emotionless emoticon that cannot possibly communicate the warmth of a smile, the wit of a smile, the danger in a smile. The word itself, "emoticon," carries an impersonal, machinelike connotation, and that's appropriate. In its transmission from human being to machine to its intended human recipient, the smile is stripped of huge amounts of data.

There is, after all, no single smile. A symbol that purports to represent all smiles in reality represents nothing at all, because it is the differences in smiles that make them matter.

A smile can be warm and inviting, or it can be a dead grin, the kind of smile where the lips make the right movement but the eyes lie silent and cold. My two daughters have smiles that suit their characters perfectly. Marv's sardonic smirk is certainly not the same as Stewie's open beam, or Boose's wry, knowing little grin. And the difference between them, well, the difference is the whole damn thing.

But resistance is futile. I once ran across an interview conducted in the 1920s, in which an older woman was waxing nostalgic about the days before the automobile sent people scurrying hither and yon.

"In the nineties, we were all much more together," she recalled. "People brought chairs and cushions out of the house and sat on the lawn. . . . We'd sit out so all evening. The younger couples perhaps would wander off for half an hour to get a soda, but they'd come back to join in the informal singing or listen while somebody strummed a mandolin or guitar."

I'm sure that when I first read that lament, I smiled a bit smugly at its charming quaintness. But I didn't quibble with its accuracy, not then and not now. I'm sure it happened just that way. In fact, in these pages I'm doing much the same thing that woman did. I'm waxing nostalgic for a passing era, and some who read these lines will probably smile—:>)—smugly at the quaintness of its message.

Change is indeed inevitable, and the world we've known today and yesterday will not be the world we confront tomorrow morning. However, accepting the inevitability of that new world doesn't mean we can't note what we lose in the transition.

It is just as I had feared. I have been taken captive, and have no hope of escape.

Breakfast à la Richard had been très wonderful: scrambled eggs, sausage, real hash browns, washed down with coffee and orange juice. But once I sat down to eat, I was doomed. This chair has grabbed me, imprisoned me, and it will not let me up. It would take a range fire to get me to move.

But that's okay. By this point, after a couple of sunbaked days on the water, isolated from the rest of the world, we've all picked up the rhythm of the river and made it our own. You can see it in our body language, hear it in our voices. We move at a deliberate, unhurried pace; any lingering hint of real-world frantic has been fried out of our bodies by the sun. When we talk, it's at a volume just barely audible above the river.

To top it off, the day ahead is a blank that we can fill any way we choose. We don't even have to pack up and move. We have nowhere we have to be, nothing we have to do, nobody we ought to call. The prospect of so much unfettered, unstructured time—"free time"—seems more luxurious and indulgent than the richest chocolate, the most expensive automobile, the most decadent restaurant meal.

The rest of the guys have decided to go fishing for a couple of hours, before the heat of the day arrives. Stewie and Alan have already gone, heading upriver together a few minutes ago. Marv and Richard are still scurrying around camp, collecting their gear. Once they're ready, they'll head off in the opposite direction, downstream.

I've decided to spend at least part of the day right here, on this chair, watching the occasional boat or raft float downstream in front of me. If I'm really feeling ambitious, I might even manage to raise my hand in greeting as they pass.

"You need anything?" Richard asks. He's standing there with Marv, both of them with fishing rods in hand, ready to take off. "I'm just asking," he continues, "because I'd hate to have it on my conscience that I went fishing and might have forced you to get out of that chair for any reason."

"Well, my aspirin bottle's right over there, and I could use a cold beer for a little later, just to wash the aspirin down."

Richard laughs, and walks over to get the aspirin. Marv starts to rummage in the cooler to get me a beer, then thinks better of it. Instead, he closes the cooler lid, grabs the handle, and drags the whole thing next to my chair, arranging it like a coffee table.

"There," he says. "That ought to hold you."

And then they're off, trudging out of the shade into the harsh sunlight, and across the desert toward the railroad tracks a few hundred yards away. Once they reach the grade, they'll walk the tracks downstream a mile or so, through a railroad tunnel carved out of the rock, and down to the next sweeping bend in the river. Then they'll start fishing their way back upstream.

That's pretty much standard procedure. Whenever we stray far from camp, we try to travel in pairs and stay within voice contact, just in case of trouble. There are many ways it could happen out here—a snakebite, a stumble. We do a lot of rock climbing, up and down cliffs, to get to some of the better fishing spots along the river, and one of the bigger hazards is the dreaded elevator rock: You put your weight on what looks to be solid footing, the rock gives way in the soft desert sand, and suddenly you're riding an express elevator down to the basement floor, and the landing ain't pretty. So traveling together is a wise precaution.

Friends have suggested that we bring walkie-talkies along with us, so that we could communicate over larger distances. It might have come in handy yesterday, for example, when I was by myself in the kayak above Whitehorse, wondering where Richard and Stew were in the main raft. Armed with radios, we would be more free to go off by ourselves in any direction we chose, and if we needed help we could just call in.

But that gets me back to the point I was trying to make earlier. I think that as communication improves—as it becomes easier for us to exchange information quickly and without cost, across barriers of time and distance—it does not bring us closer. It pushes us further apart.

To put it in bumper-sticker terms, communication displaces community.

I'll concede that sounds like a contradiction. If we can communicate more easily, surely that ought to enrich community. You know, the global village and all that. The two words, "communication" and "community," even share the same Latin root, *communis,* or "common."

But they share that root for a reason. Communication has long been one of the primary reasons that community exists. Throughout history, part of the reason that we have sought each other's company has been to exchange information.

On the savannas of Africa, being sociable gave us a great competitive advantage. It allowed us to share important data: Where is the best hunting? How do you make a spearhead? How do you set a broken bone? Can you help me?

The founders of Western civilization, the ancient Greeks, defined a city as the number of people that could be assembled in one place within sound of a human voice. As that example demonstrates, mass communication isn't anything new. Its form has just changed. Before television or printing presses, it meant a crowd listening to a speech, or a congregation joining in worship. It meant people getting together. Before video or DVD, you had to go to a movie house with hundreds of other people to see a film, and before movies you had to go to a play, surrounded by your fellow human beings, watching live human actors on stage.

Technology has rendered community less essential. It allows us to acquire information without the hassle of face-to-face interaction. It has replaced a strong form of communication—communication about who we are as people, as individuals—with a weak form of communication that transmits merely data.

It's less of a bother to call someone than to meet him in person. It's easier to leave a voice mail message than to have a phone conversation. It's more efficient still to send someone an e-mail, because that way you don't have to talk at all. You don't have to invest the time and energy.

And though the five of us have never discussed it, I think that's why we don't bring walkie-talkies to the river. We all know it wouldn't be right. Yes, I could be talking right now to Richard and Marv as they hike down the railway line, or to Alan and Stew as they fish upstream from here. I could have that noise blaring in my ear, and have my noise blaring in someone else's ear. But why?

Sure, with that technology at our fingertips, we would be less reliant on each other and could wander anywhere we wished. We might even catch more fish by doing so.

But what's our real purpose in being out here? We already catch a lot of fish; a mindless commitment to catch even more, aided and abetted by technology, wouldn't make us any happier.

But catching a fish on the first cast, when Stewart's right around the corner to hear you whoop with excitement, or when Alan and Marv happen to be floating by in front of you watching, well, that's the fun part. Bragging about the great fish you just landed wouldn't be the same if you did it over the radio waves, rather than in person, with the fish as evidence. If you're going to do it that way, the other person might as well be back in Nashville.

In the real world, the cell phone presents the same set of trade-offs as walkie-talkies would out here. Because the cell phone allows us to contact almost anybody, almost anywhere, at almost any time, it frees us from having to maintain that contact by more personal, intimate means. So while we might think that the cell phone connects us more closely, in reality it encourages us to separate.

Some of the best evidence of communication's corrosive effect on community has come from the business world. Thanks to the Internet and e-mail and other technologies, corporations have been able to pare their organizations down to their core functions, outsourcing secondary functions such as accounting, human resources, and even manufacturing. Nike, for instance, doesn't own a single facility to manufacture shoes or apparel. Instead, it uses communications technology to manage a network of contract factories in places such as Vietnam and Indonesia, far from its headquarters in Beaverton, Oregon.

Workers in turn have been "liberated" from lifetime or even long-term employment with a single company, and now compete in

a workforce increasingly typified by temporary and contract workers who have no loyalty or ties. The average employee entering the
workforce today is told to expect half a dozen careers—not jobs, but
careers—before reaching retirement age. And telecommuting allows
many workers to operate from home, where they rarely interact in
person with their colleagues.

In each of these cases, improved communication probably
enhanced business productivity, but it did not bring people
closer together. To the contrary, the efficiency it creates in an economic sense comes at the cost of eroding the bonds that once
linked worker to employer, worker to worker, and employer to
community.

Those links, now broken, did more than transmit information—
they also served a psychic and social need. Human beings enjoy
feeling like a part of something larger than themselves. It's an emotional demand that has been bred into our genes. So even after sharing information electronically, we're left still yearning for
community. We thirst for it. It's part of being human.

Ironically, that yearning for contact, for relationships, inevitably
deepens in times of stress, when instinct tells us to pull closer
together. Research proves that people who have strong social networks cope better with anxiety than those who try to cope on their
own. So while communication accelerates the pace and stress of
modern life, it also dismantles the community that serves as our
most natural and effective refuge from that stress. It's the dreaded
double whammy.

Communication can even corrode that most intimate of human
communities, the family. Jagdish Sheth, a marketing professor at
Emory University in Atlanta, notes the emergence of what he calls
"the roommate family"—family members who relate to each other
no more often, and with no more intimacy, than roommates who
share a common dwelling and mailing address. He sees it as an

emerging model in Western society, and it seems to me that he may be right.

In a roommate family, each family member lives in his or her own space, or bedroom; their lives intersect only if they happen to run across each other in common areas such as the kitchen. To a large degree, that lifestyle has been enabled by technology. Various surveys report that between two-thirds and three-quarters of American teenagers now have a television in their bedroom, and the number is rising quickly. Many also own a cell phone. Increasing numbers also own a bedroom computer, with more than half of those connected to the Internet. Today, between 85 and 95 percent of children's TV viewing occurs with no parent in the room.

In the future—a future not too distant—the typical American bedroom will be equipped with a television with a cable hookup, a computer linked to the Internet, a telephone, a game system, and a stereo system. We're all building our own personal Situation Rooms. So on a typical evening, Junior will be in his room playing Doom, Sis will be on her own computer "instant-messaging" with her circle of friends, and Dad will be sitting alone in the ill-named "family room," staring at a basketball game on his big-screen satellite TV, while Mom watches a Lifetime channel movie on a separate set in the master bedroom.

The glue of the roommate family, the means by which critical information is shared among its members, is no longer the evening meal, where they all sit at the same table at the same time. It's been replaced by the cell phone, which after all is more efficient and doesn't require the feat of scheduling four busy people at one location simultaneously. Some families even issue Palm Pilots to each member, so their individual schedules can be coordinated electronically. Rather than bring people together, technology enables them to separate.

Is technology, then, the cause of the decay of the family as an institution? Does it explain the high divorce rate, the rising rate of childbirth outside of marriage, the decline in two-parent households that has so alarmed religious leaders and social observers?

No, of course not. But we do live in a culture that celebrates the individual and denigrates the group—and responsibility to the group—as a drag on the individual's autonomy. So we create technology to enhance that autonomy, to make that individualistic way of life more productive and comfortable. The problem is not technology, but the goals we use it to achieve.

It's naive to think that the family as an institution could somehow be immune to that corrosive trend, that we can abandon and discredit every other sense of obligation to each other as old-fashioned and inefficient while preserving family obligations intact. In fact, while I've never seen any numbers on it, I'd be willing to bet that the typical family today spends less time communicating face-to-face than at any point in the history of the institution.

Because communication breaks down community.

In his 1964 classic *Understanding Media,* Marshall McLuhan related the story of several postwar Indian villages where a United Nations relief agency had installed pipes to deliver running water to each home. After a few months, according to McLuhan, the village elders went to relief-agency officials and asked that the pipes be ripped out.

The elders had realized that nobody congregated any longer at the village well, where they used to wait in line to fill their water jugs. The well had traditionally been the communal center of village life, the place where gossip was exchanged and village values were reinforced. It was the place where the village met to connect its dots and create a mutual sense of narrative and identity. With running water delivered to each home, the well could no longer serve that essential purpose.

Oddly, McLuhan himself did not appreciate the full metaphorical power of that anecdote. He offered it merely to demonstrate that traditional cultures are more sensitive to technological impact than Western societies, and more likely to recognize the changes that technology imposes. But changes in the media industry since 1964 have made the story more subtle and rich in meaning.

In McLuhan's time, the media were still mass media. There were only three major broadcast networks in the United States, so on Saturday night, for example, everyone watched *The Ed Sullivan Show*. Radio had not yet fragmented into strict demographic formats, so the nation's number one song would still be recognized by young and old, rich and poor, black and white and brown. Mass-circulation magazines such as *Life* constituted the culture's common reading material.

In such an environment, McLuhan's concept of the world as a "global village" drawing data and information from the same communal well seemed to make perfect sense.

But if we are a global village today, it is a village in which the communal well has been abandoned; each of us now has his or her own personal info-delivery pipeline. That is, I think, the source of much of the free-floating anxiety in Western culture. We sense that we have cut ourselves off from each other. We're out there alone in the desert with a walkie-talkie, but with no one nearby.

And if it's a little frightening for us Americans, to more traditional cultures these times must be terrifying. We in the West think of globalization in terms of lowering trade barriers, and expanding wealth and commerce. Those in Africa, Asia, and the Middle East— and to some degree in Europe as well—experience it in more traumatic terms. They understand that to participate in globalization, to become its beneficiaries rather than its victims, they will have to abandon the collectivist values that have long been at the core of their cultures and their way of seeing the world.

It places them in a terrible dilemma. The more frightening the world becomes, the more instinctively they want to turn to the group for comfort and support. But the deeper they burrow into collectivism, the more difficult it becomes to see a place for themselves in a world that demands individualism as its price of participation.

In fact, it is tempting to conclude that communal societies, communal values, and communal ways of looking at the world will all but disappear in the century to come, replaced in every culture by a technologically enhanced hyperindividualism. It's hard to comprehend how people who think and behave in communal terms can compete against those of us who believe that the needs and desires of the individual should take precedence, particularly now that our advantages have been so enhanced by technology.

But think for a moment about the enormity of that change: A fundamental way of life and thinking that has nurtured human beings from our earliest days as a species, that shaped our evolution genetically, culturally, and in religious terms, may now be passing from the earth, and in fact could disappear entirely within our lifetimes.

It will not go quietly.

I struggle to my feet, fighting against the stiffness. I have to pace. It's what I do when my mind starts taking me to unfamiliar, uncomfortable places. I get physically antsy. I need to move, even if it hurts.

It's so damn quiet. With the departure of Marv and Richard the campsite has become absurdly quiet. It's as if no human voice had ever been heard in this space. I can hear the water flowing, the wind blowing, yet the silence is almost overwhelming.

I walk upstream a bit, watching the river flow by, my eye drawn instinctively to movement as a fish leaps from the water about twenty feet from shore. Out in the desert, on the opposite shore, a dust devil rises up, spinning dirt and dust in a column thirty or forty feet high. The swallows have come out too, darting above the water, chasing the same insect prey that has drawn the fish out of their inactivity.

I'm walking, pacing, nervous and disturbed because my reveries have brought me an image of those two airplanes, of watching them crash into the World Trade Center towers that fine September morning, of the towers tumbling down, of the horror of that day.

The genesis of those attacks lies somewhere in the desperation of a people cornered by history.

People of a religion and a culture that stress loyalty over individualism, people whose story is that of the communal not the personal, people who know that they cannot change as the world requires and still be what they know themselves to be.

People who see the water rising behind the dam, and see the falls beginning to disappear.

And so they attack, blindly, stupidly.

I pick up a rock and try to toss it into the river, but it's a feeble throw. I'm too stiff and sore to give it a real fling.

I don't think that nineteen men of a culture that celebrates the individual could have sacrificed themselves so willingly, with such cold-blooded certainty. Nor could they have killed so many others— so many innocents—with such ugly callousness to the stories they were ending.

But, of course, using planes as bombs wasn't an entirely new concept. The Japanese, another communal culture, had turned to suicide pilots in flying bombs—the kamikazes—to destroy American ships in World War II.

But it's telling, I think, that the kamikazes didn't emerge until late in the war, as an act of desperation once the Japanese realized that American ships, planes, and troops would soon converge on the home islands. In the early days of the war, when the outcome was still unclear, kamikazes had not even been contemplated as a military weapon.

Once the war ended, the Japanese decided to embrace the tactics of their conqueror, at least after a fashion. They created a hybrid form of capitalism that on the surface seemed to operate much like our own, yet retained many of the group loyalties that had always marked their culture. Companies hired employees for life, Japanese companies cooperated rather than competed with each other, and Japanese consumers showed great loyalty to higher-priced Japanese goods, spurning whatever lower-priced imports were allowed in by the government. In the decades that followed World War II, Japan grew into one of the world's major economic powers, and by 1990 the coming world dominance of Japan's economy was a standard theme of the business press.

Since then, though, Japan's economy has faltered badly. The introduction of personal computers, cell phones, and the Internet put an even greater emphasis on the individual, and made it more difficult to sustain a communal approach. The Japanese, like the Soviet Union, could not compete. They would not give up the protections of the group and make themselves, or each other, vulnerable as individuals. It violated their cultural norms. As a result, they have become vulnerable as a group.

I need to keep walking, to work this through. I decide to change direction, to hike downstream and see what adventures Richard and Marv might be having. A good walk is what I need, to stretch out the kinks.

Before heading out, I swing back by camp for a few minutes to pack a little knapsack with ice and a six-pack. I leave my fishing gear behind. I still don't feel confident enough in my legs to start clambering up and down the steep riverbanks downstream.

I take the trail out of camp, walking slowly up a gentle ridgeline until I'm about a hundred feet above the river. Sometimes from this vantage point you can watch as trout position themselves in the clear river down below, taking shelter from the current behind large rocks. This is what the river must look like to an osprey, hovering high over the water with its wings outstretched, searching for prey. But unlike an osprey, which comes equipped by nature with a special set of lenses, we humans need a good pair of sunglasses to cut through the steely glare of the sun on the water.

As I look downstream to where we'll be heading tomorrow, I can see the landscape beginning to change. From this point on, the river cuts through the Mutton Mountains, named after the wild sheep that lived here until, in a fate similar to that of the Native Americans afflicted by smallpox, they fell prey to disease introduced by domesticated sheep.

The canyons will deepen and narrow in the days ahead; the mesas and bluffs that marked the more open upper river will disappear. The white water will also become more challenging.

As I walk, I keep a sharp eye on the riverbank below. Marv and Richard could be anywhere, hidden among the overhanging alders that line the bank. The trout love to hide under those trees, taking shelter from the sun and from any osprey that might be hovering overhead. The trees are also thick with caddis flies, dusky little mothlike creatures that hatch out of the water and serve as the primary food source for these fish. The caddis is the meat and potatoes of the Deschutes redside trout.

After a mile or so of walking, the soreness seems to be working its way out of my legs, but it's also hot out here on this ridge, exposed to the brutal desert sun. The ice in my backpack is melting, sending a welcome trickle of cold water down my back.

Suddenly I see a bit of movement in the trees about a quarter mile ahead, and a blur of color as well. It's Richard's red cap. I look up and down the bank—no sign of Marv, but he's got to be near here as well.

I hike until I'm directly above Richard's spot, then yell down to him.

"Hey man, doing any good?"

"What the hell you doing out here? I thought you had to hold that chair down all day."

"Oh, feeling a little feistier, thought I'd take a stroll. Figured you hardworking fishermen might like an ice-cold beer by now."

"Oh man, that sounds great. I'm coming up, let me make one more cast."

I smile to myself. He's trying to catch one while I'm watching.

"Marv around?"

"Yeah, I passed him about ten minutes ago a little farther back. I bet if you hollered he'd hear you. He should be coming this way pretty soon."

I look downstream. Still no sign of the Big Swede. But there's a nice little shady area a little farther down, a place tucked into the trees where the three of us could sit awhile. Staying up here and having a beer in the desert blast furnace would be foolish.

"I'm gonna climb down to that shady spot right downstream from you," I yell down to Richard. "We can wait for Marv there."

I see Richard nod his head, so I start walking the ridge again, this time looking for a likely route down the rocks to the river below. Once I find one, I start picking my way down the cliff. I can feel Richard's watchful eyes on me as I descend. It's hell being the wounded one.

A few minutes later I've found a very pleasant little perch on a rock down in the trees, right by the water. I've shucked off the knapsack, and Richard has joined me in the shade. We've just cracked open our beer cans when we hear a rock bouncing our way. It's Marv; he's hiking upstream along the lower trail, about fifteen feet up the bank from where we sit, concealed in the trees.

"I don't think he knows we're here," Richard whispers. "He threw that rock to check for snakes."

I nod my head in silent agreement.

A few seconds later we catch a glimpse of Marv, hiking fast along the trail. Just as he moves past us, Richard puts his tongue to the top of his mouth and makes a sound remarkably like that of a rattle.

Marv stops dead in his tracks, glancing around, his back to us. He doesn't know where the sound came from. I reach down and pick up a little stone, about the size of a quarter, and toss it into the sagebrush a couple of feet to Marv's left.

Instantly, Marv's head swivels, his eyes now fixated on the spot where the rock landed. He starts slowly backing off the trail toward the river, his eyes still fixed on the spot in the brush. Suddenly he loses his footing and tumbles backward.

A few seconds later, he's sitting on his butt, in the river, right in front of us. He looks over at me, then at Richard, and I'm sure that our startled delight is hard to miss.

"Want a beer?" Richard deadpans as he digs into the knapsack.

"Maybe later. First, though, I have to kill you both."

About an hour later, when the three of us finally climb back up the cliff to the rim trail, the heat has truly become oppressive, reflecting off the rocks and dirt. It's hard to describe how bright it is out here this time of day. It takes about twenty minutes of trudging to make it back to the campsite, and by then we're roasted. Baste us with garlic and butter and we'd make a fine meal. During that whole long march we hadn't said a word to each other, just put our heads down and walked, but now we all seem to be of one mind.

Marv and Richard shuck their fishing gear, I dump off the knapsack, and we all head to the boats, where our life jackets are stored.

A few minutes later, life jackets strapped to our chests, the three of us are hiking upstream a ways, to the point where the water rushing out of Whitehorse suddenly deepens and slows into a large, inviting pool.

We walk out into the water—the extremely cold water. Marv dives in first, then Richard. I stand there, summoning my courage, and then dive in, headfirst. I feel my testicles shrink up into my body, seeking refuge from the cold, and I gasp at the shock. It's so cold it literally takes your breath away.

And then it feels absolutely perfect.

I lie back in my life jacket and let the current pull me into the pool and swing me around in a large circular eddy. You could float out here for hours, just letting the water do with you what it will.

We call this a Marv, in honor of our colleague who initiated the practice. It's a remarkable thing. After a few minutes out here, the sun-induced stupor has disappeared; the blood in my brain has cooled, and I can think clearly again. My seared skin feels cool and rejuvenated.

We talk quietly as we float, about the menu for dinner tonight, about cutting open the extra cooler tomorrow morning and restocking ice before we leave, about the fishing spots in the next stretch of river. A few minutes later, Alan and Stewie hike back into camp, and they too eagerly shed their fishing gear and join us in the river.

Then Stewie, floating about fifty feet away from me, speaks up loudly, his voice carrying across the water.

"Hey, guys, look at this," he says, and he plucks a piece of clothing out of the water. Then he points upstream. A half-sunken cooler is bobbing toward us, with a gallon milk jug and other debris in its wake.

We all know immediately what that means: Somebody's dumped it up in Whitehorse. And not just a kayak, but a whole boat or raft, full of supplies. Stewie dog-paddles over to the cooler, stows the shirt and milk inside, and starts kicking his way toward shore, dragging the cooler behind him. The rest of us make for shore as well.

Other items—pieces of clothing mainly—are now coming down the chute. Oh boy, here comes somebody's sleeping bag. That's not going to make for a pleasant evening.

And way upriver, too far to make out clearly, some strange kind of craft is slowly making its way downstream. From here it looks almost like one of those Civil War ironclads, with a low profile and a smokestack sticking out of the middle.

"What the hell . . . ?"

"I don't know. Never seen anything like that before, but I think it's moving this way. Those are people I see on it, right?"

"Yeah, I guess so. They must be the guys who dumped it. It's the only boat in sight."

Boose and I splash back into the water to fetch the sleeping bag and other debris, while the other three guys shed their life jackets and start walking upstream, driven by curiosity.

About ten minutes later, the investigating party returns. Boose and I have unrolled the sleeping bag and have each grabbed an end, twisting it hard to squeeze the water out of it. The craft has gotten quite a bit closer now, and from a distance of a hundred feet it looks like something fabricated by people trying to escape from a desert island.

It's made up of five or six very large inner tubes, all lashed together with ropes and bungee cords. A piece of thick marine plywood serves as a deck, and at the center of the craft are two fifty-five-gallon metal drums, standing straight up, where I guess they stow their gear.

Three people are on board: a woman in her late twenties, who seems to be in charge, and two guys about the same age. She looks grim and pretty pissed, yelling out orders as the three of them paddle the craft through the last remaining boulders before they hit the shelter of the calm eddy.

By the time they get to shore, we've dragged what gear we could recover over to their landing area. Richard has launched the kayak and is paddling around with a fishing net, scooping out food items and clothing caught in the eddy.

There's an awkward silence as they hit the bank. Marv and Alan drag the boat onto shore and tie it off to a tree stump.

"Everybody all right?" Alan asks.

"Shit. Yeah, we're fine," the girl says. Her bedraggled companions don't say a word. The two of them stumble ashore and collapse onto the rocks, still a little stunned, like lost souls. They look as though they've been whipped and sent to bed without supper. Looking at them, I realize that I probably looked the same way about this time yesterday.

"We flipped it about halfway down," the girl says, making the necessary explanation as succinct as possible. "We got pinned against a rock, and then the water caught us and turned us over."

She reaches down into a barrel and comes up with a soggy mass of something in her hand.

"Everything's wet. Shit."

She starts flinging wet clothing and gear out of the barrel and onto shore. The two guys still sit there, staring out at the river. The only sound is the crashing of the water through Whitehorse and the plopping of wet clothing and foodstuffs as they smack against the rocks.

It's a little awkward.

"Well, let us know if you need anything," Marv finally says, and we melt away, leaving them to sulk in privacy.

Back in our own campsite, the new arrivals are the topic of conversation. We can see them clearly from our little shelter in the trees, and we're keeping an eye on what's happening, trying not to be too obvious about it. It's beginning to look like a yard sale over there, with equipment and clothing scattered all over the bank.

The two guys have finally roused themselves, and have begun wringing out their other two sleeping bags and hanging them over rocks and sagebrush to dry. In most places they'd have no hope of sleeping dry and warm tonight, but out here, with a few more hours of 110-degree heat and a good breeze blowing, they've got a chance.

Already my shorts are bone-dry, and I've been out of the water for only ten minutes.

"Look, they just pulled out a stove. They've still got that anyway."

"What about food? You think they've got much left? It sure looked like everything got soaked."

"They could always eat fish."

"Yeah, but I didn't see any fishing gear."

"Maybe they lost it overboard."

"No. I didn't see any gear at all. They don't seem the fishermen type."

"Hey, Richard, you think we got enough food to feed them tonight?"

"Not from what's on the menu. But we could go fishing. I bet it wouldn't take us long to catch enough to feed everybody. We could cook up some rice too, we've got plenty of that."

"Yeah. We could send our bachelor over to invite them. You'd like that, wouldn't you, Alan?"

Alan's the only one of us who's not married. Well, that's not technically true. Richard's been married twice, but like I said, he's sworn off women for the time being.

"We're just offering them some help in their time of need," Marv says. "Besides, Alan, she's kinda pretty when she's mad."

This is ridiculous. We're grown men, acting like a bunch of seventh-graders trying to push one of our friends into asking a girl to dance.

"Yeah, she's pretty, for sure," Alan says. "But don't you think she's with one of them?"

"It looks to me like they're just friends," says Stew. "I don't see any sign of romance in that crowd."

"Plus they look like hippies," Richard says. "With your long hair, Alan, you'd fit right in."

Alan, thereby deputized by his peers, grabs four beers as icebreakers and heads back over to the yard sale. We can see him talking, at first with just the girl, then with all three of them. The beers seem welcome, and from a distance at least their mood seems to have improved. There's a bit of laughter, and gestures of agreement— heads nodding up and down, hand shaking—before Alan turns and walks back our way.

"Three extra for dinner," he says with a grin as he comes out of the bright sunlight and under the trees. "They lost their propane for the stove. I told them we'd feed 'em tonight, and could probably spare them a can or two of propane before we leave tomorrow."

"What's the deal with the homemade boat? I've never seen anything like that in my life," says Marv, who's been coming down this river since he was a kid. He guided us all through the white water here the first year, when none of the rest of us knew what we were doing.

"She says that when she was a kid, her dad used to bring her family down here on a raft like that. She and her friends came over the mountains from Eugene and put it together at the launch ramp."

"Eugene, huh? Like that's a surprise."

Eugene, about a hundred miles to the southwest, on the wet side of the mountains, is the site of the University of Oregon. It also happens to be one of the last remaining refuges of hippies and, in this case, neo-hippies, their spiritual children and grandchildren.

"They need anything else right now?"

"No. They're just drying everything out. Her name is Sunny, by the way."

"Oh. And who are the guys with her?"

"Well, I guess I didn't catch their names," Boose says, smiling again. "Looks to me like they're just friends."

"So what are we feeding, eight people?" says Richard, eager for a project. "I'm going to stay here and get things going. J-Book, you up for fishing, or you still on the injured list?"

I tell him I'm ready to fish. I may not look it yet, but I'm actually feeling close to normal.

"Okay, so that means eight people to feed, four of you fishing . . . we need eight fish—two each."

The camp is suddenly energized. Everybody has a mission, bustling around, getting ready to depart. It's late afternoon, and the fish will start to get active again pretty soon.

This is a rare occurrence. We almost never fish for meat, although legally you're allowed to keep two fish a day, each between ten and thirteen inches. Fish that are any larger have already gotten big enough to breed, so you have to let them go. Besides, a foot-long fish is the perfect size for a frying pan.

Since they fished the upstream portion this morning, Alan and Stewie announce they're headed downstream. Marv and I gear up and head the other way. We wave as we pass Camp Sunny—they have everything stretched out under the sun now, and are just wandering around, turning things as they dry. The boys don't look quite so downtrodden.

A little bit up the trail, as we walk in silence, I take the opportunity I've been waiting for. I know what the response is going to be, but what the hell, I'm throwing it out there anyway.

"You know, Alan told me what you did yesterday, running up here because you thought I was in trouble," I say. "Thanks, man."

"Shit. I was just trying to get upstream so I could laugh at you, you dumb shit."

Like I said, I knew what to expect.

"So, just a little entertainment, huh?"

Marv starts to laugh, until a sudden noise off to our left brings us both to a halt. An ungodly screeching is coming from the sagebrush just a few feet off the trail, and as we stand there, trying to figure out what the hell's going on, a ball of dust about two feet high comes rolling out of the brush and into the open.

We step back, startled, and instinctively point our fishing rods toward the dust ball to keep it from rolling our way.

At first, it's hard to believe what we're seeing. It's like nothing I've ever encountered or even heard of. A ball of dust making a hellacious noise. I stare at this thing, dumbstruck, until I realize that inside all that dust there must be something alive.

The dust is so thick, though, that you can't penetrate it. The thing continues to roll right across our trail—at most, you can catch a brief glimpse of brown or gray fur through the dust. And the noise coming out of there is incredible.

Suddenly it hits me: It looks like . . . strange as it seems, it looks exactly like one of those fight scenes out of an old cartoon, with a cloud of dust obscuring the combatants, and once in a while a fist or arm protruding.

Then everything falls quiet.

As the dust cloud settles, I make out a ferret, about a foot long, staring straight at the two of us with eyes so fierce they chill me to the bone. The ferret's ribs are heaving from the exertion of combat, and in its mouth it holds the snout of a ground squirrel. In fact, the ferret's mouth is open so wide that it completely covers the squirrel's nose and mouth. The squirrel is all but dead now, suffocated. Its only movement is an occasional twitch.

The ferret lies there, panting, staring up at us as if daring us to try to steal its prey. Personally, I don't want a piece of that bad little mother, no thank you very much.

We back off another step or two, and the ferret begins to back away as well, its eyes never leaving ours, until it disappears tail first down a hole hidden next to a rock. The last thing we see is the life-less tail of the squirrel, following its conqueror down into the earth.

Marv and I turn to each other, jaws agape.

"Animal Planet!"

"Did you see that? Teeth like a Doberman!"

"That thing's so mean it would kick a Doberman's butt, man! I wish I had a camera; the guys aren't gonna believe this."

"Was that a squirrel? That was some sort of squirrel it had, right?"

"Did you see how the ferret grabbed it? Right over its mouth. It cut off his air supply. Did you know they killed that way?"

I shake my head no. The image of the ferret, staring into our eyes with such fury, is going to stay with me a long time, I expect. I feel as though I've just been out on the Serengeti in Africa, watching a lion bring down a zebra. When you see the ferocity of a life-and-death struggle play out just a few feet in front of you, the size of the participants doesn't really matter.

That's part of the cruel beauty of places like this. Things out here have consequences. Either you succeed or you fail, and if you fail, there's no hitting the replay button and starting over. I have a gash in my shin to prove it.

We resume our hike, still talking and shaking our heads in disbelief. To our right, the lower part of Whitehorse rages and foams. As we walk, we keep an eye along the bank, looking for equipment that might have washed ashore from our neighbors' raft.

"I'm gonna try right over there, Marv, down behind that rock," I tell him.

"Looks fishy to me," he says, peering down the steep incline. "I'll go on up ahead. If you limit out, come find me. And hey—look out for killer ferrets."

"Yeah, yeah."

I roll a snake-check rock down the hill, then pick my way down the bank to my fishing spot. The boulders are almost hot to the touch, radiating heat stored up from a day of intense bright August sunlight.

The water sounds alive rushing through here, and I don't know why, but it's very soothing. Someone should come tape this sound and market it for those white-noise machines, the ones that allow you to select from birdsongs or crashing surf or midnight rain.

"Deschutes Serenade," they could call it.

John C. Frémont, with Kit Carson as his scout, led an expedition up this valley in the winter of 1843–44, headed south from the Columbia to California. In its journals, the Frémont party called this the Falls River, the English translation of the name given it by French trappers, Des Chutes.

"In all our journeying we had never travelled a country where the rivers were so abounding in falls, and the name of this stream is singularly characteristic," Frémont wrote in his entry for December 5. "At every place where we come in the neighborhood of the river is heard the roaring of the falls."

Frémont was an odd duck, though. For reasons that historians can't fully explain, he brought a small cannon with him on that wilderness expedition, dragging it over mountains, across rivers, and over hundreds of miles of roadless desert. It never served a military purpose—using a cannon against the scattered bands of Indians they encountered would have been ridiculous. According to expedition journals, though, they did occasionally fire the cannon at buffalo, just for the cruel sport of watching a cannonball smash into the majestic beast and knock it to the ground.

I've reached the riverbank now and wade into the water, splashing through the shoals to the spot I had seen from up above. The cold water feels good again on my battered legs.

This is not the slow, deep water that we would normally fish, when we're looking for the big ones. This is where the smaller trout—the ones suitable for dinner—tend to hang out. After about four casts, I hook my first keeper, a nice fat twelve-incher. As it splashes toward me, bouncing off the rocks in its frenzy to get free, I can't help but think about that squirrel, fighting for its life against the ferret.

I grasp the fish in my hand and carefully disengage the hook from its mouth. You have to be careful—a thrashing fish can bury a hook deep in your hand. Then, holding the fish by the tail, I whack it two or three times, hard, against a rock, until it ceases to struggle.

Almost immediately, the bright, vibrant colors fade from its body. This taking of life to sustain your own—it's a reality you sometimes forget if you do all your foraging in a grocery store. Those cellophaned packages of red meat, the fillets of fish at the seafood counter, are more than prepackaged pieces of protein. They too once lived, although more and more of those fish are being raised like cattle, in sea ranches, fed on pellets.

I stuff the trout into a carry bag dangling from my waist, then glance around, looking for a likely spot where another trout might be lurking. Across the river, on the reservation side, I notice a pickup truck towing a fishing boat. A column of dust marks its route over a rough desert road; it appears to be headed this way, toward the river.

I know who it is. In the last few years, a couple of Warm Springs Indians have opened guide services, offering nontribal fishermen the chance to fish legally in waters where only reservation members could previously cast a line. The guides don't market their businesses very aggressively, but maybe that's on purpose. They probably have all the customers they want. This guy's bringing some clients for some evening fly-fishing in the calm waters down below here, opposite our campsite.

I cast again, farther out into the water this time, and watch as the truck comes to a stop directly across from me. Doors swing open and three occupants climb out: a man and a woman, looking as though they just walked out of the L.L. Bean catalog, and their pot-bellied guide, dressed in blue jeans, sneakers, and T-shirt. As the guide walks briskly to the boat, leaning over to pull out two fly rods already rigged for action, his clients stand there motionless, like two mannequins, awaiting instructions on what to do next.

The guide hands each of them a rod and points to the river, assigning each of them a stretch of water.

Initially, some tribal members had objected to the idea of opening their side of the river to outsiders, and for good reason. They and other tribal groups have had to struggle for centuries to defend their communal sense of identity against forces far more powerful than themselves. Given that history, they are understandably suspicious about any proposal that would convert their commonly held property to private use.

In the nineteenth century, for example, the British army tried to destroy the social structure of coastal Canadian tribes by banning potlatch, the ritual in which individuals would sponsor a feast and give away everything they owned to their fellow tribe members, enhancing their social standing by reducing themselves to poverty. The British understood that potlatch reinforced the tribal cohesiveness that made the Native Americans so difficult to absorb. It supplied what every important communal institution provides, a sense of security in being bound to others, and a sense of status among peers.

The U.S. government made its own concerted attempts to destroy tribal connections and identity, and for the same reasons. Well into the twentieth century, it would forcibly remove Indian children from their families and ship them to far-off schools where their hair would be cut, they were forbidden to speak their native languages or practice their religions, and they were indoctrinated into the ways of the white man. Jim Thorpe, the great athlete and a graduate of the Carlisle Indian School, was a product of that system.

Like the British Canadians, American officials also understood the importance of property in reinforcing tribal identity. Through the Dawes Act of 1887, the federal government stripped the tribes of much of their communally held property, allocating it instead to individual Indians in 160-acre parcels. As U.S. senator Henry Dawes of Massachusetts explained the theory, "The common field is the seat of barbarism, while the separate farm is the door to civilization."

By 1901, President Teddy Roosevelt lauded the Dawes Act as "a mighty pulverizing engine to break up the tribal mass," and he was right. By the 1930s, more than two-thirds of the land that had been communally held by Native Americans in 1887 had been allotted to individual Indians and in turn lost forever to the white man.

The final spasm of Indian resistance, at least in its physical form, ended with the infamous massacre of the Sioux at the Pine Ridge Reservation in 1890. A member of the Northern Paiute, one of the tribes that now live across the way, played a major role in that tragedy.

Wovoka, born down in Nevada, was a Paiute prophet who by the late 1870s was traveling the West, roaming from tribe to tribe. At one point in his wanderings he made it as far north as the Columbia River, which means he almost certainly visited his fellow Paiute here on the Warm Springs reservation.

Eventually, Wovoka began to preach that the Great Spirit had come to him in a vision, telling him how to rid the continent of the white man and restore things to their natural order. If the tribes would unite, if they would reject the white man and his civilization, including alcohol, farming, firearms, and other technology, if they would reembrace the traditional way of life then on the brink of disappearing, the Great Spirit would once again smile upon the Indian, Wovoka promised. The buffalo would return, as would their Native American ancestors, and their white oppressors would disappear.

Wovoka also promised that those who performed the Ghost Dance that he had been taught by the Great Spirit, and who donned specially prepared ghost shirts, would be made immune to the white man's bullets.

The new religion spread quickly among a desperate people, finding particular resonance among the Sioux, who had sent representatives to Wovoka to hear of his vision. The growing popularity of the Ghost Dance so frightened government agents on the Pine Ridge Reservation in South Dakota that they tried to ban it. When Sitting Bull and the other Sioux refused to accept the ban, reservation agents summoned the army.

The movement ended shortly thereafter in the massacre of almost three hundred Lakota Sioux, many of them unarmed, many of them wearing ghost shirts, at a place called Wounded Knee.

A similar but even more heartbreaking story played out in South Africa in the mid-nineteenth century. A girl in the Xhosa clan, the same group that later gave birth to Nelson Mandela, was told in a vision that if the tribe killed all their cattle and destroyed all of their crops, their ancestors would return from the dead and lead them in driving off the white invader.

In their desperation, the Xhosa began slaughtering thousands of their own cattle and burning acres and acres of crops, the source of their wealth and sustenance. Instead of freedom, though, the sacrifice produced mass starvation, and destroyed what little had remained of the Xhosa's ability to resist the white takeover.

The kamikazes, the attack on the Twin Towers, the Ghost Dance, and the Great Cattle Slaughter are to varying degrees all acts of resistance by communal societies fighting for survival. They also share a common result, which is failure. Today, places such as the Warm Springs community across the river serve as reservations not just for the surviving remnants of the Native Americans who once dominated this continent, but for the last vestiges of communal society in this country.

And what is true of this country almost inevitably becomes true for the rest of the world as well.

"Yo! You still fishing?" Marv calls out from above.

I feel a tug on my line.

"Not anymore!"

"You lucky son of a bitch."

"Luck has nothing to do with it," I yell back at him, never taking my eyes off the fish as I bring it to hand.

A half hour later Marv and I are walking back into camp, each with our limit of two fish. Even from a hundred yards away, we can hear Stewie and Richard laughing and carrying on.

"Uh-oh," says Marv with a grin. "I think Richard's gotten into his whiskey a little early."

When we walk into camp, there's another surprise. Sunny is sitting in my chair and having a beer. One of her friends is there as well.

Alan jumps up from his chair next to Sunny and makes the introductions.

"Guys, this is Sunny, Sunny Rollins. And this is her friend Pete. And Pete, Sunny, this is my brother Jay, and this is Marv."

"Sunny Rollins?" I ask. "Like the saxophone player?"

"Well, Sunny's not my real first name," she says, smiling. "My dad's a jazz fan, and he just started calling me that."

I can see why. When she smiles, she lights up the canyon. Julia Roberts has nothing on this woman. It's an aspect of her that we hadn't seen earlier, when she was still flinging wet clothes to the ground. She's added a purple paisley wraparound skirt to her purple bathing-suit top since then, and it adds up to a real earthmother thing that . . . well, let's just say that Alan has a weakness for that.

Marv, though, is excited just to have a new audience. As I turn to put away my fishing gear, I hear him launch into the first of what are sure to be many retellings of "The Tale of the Ferocious Ferret," delivering it with all the bombast of a traveling Shakespearean trouper.

By the time I store my equipment, grab a beer, and get back to the story circle, the dust ball has just disappeared and the villain, the wily ferret, has emerged with its hapless victim. The audience seems rapt, so I sidle over to Richard standing at the stove.

"So, how do you want the fish cleaned? Heads and tails off, or the whole fish?"

"Whole fish. Trout amandine, ce soir, monsieur." And he taps his finger on a bag of slivered almonds sitting next to the stove.

"My God. You come prepared for anything."

Richard smiles. I could not have offered him higher praise. I grab the eight trout sitting in a cooler and head for the riverbank. One summer during my college years I worked at a fish wholesaler on the docks in Plymouth, Massachusetts, and got to be pretty handy cleaning fish, so it's become one of my designated duties. I don't mind; it goes pretty quickly. Catch the fish, clean the fish, eat the fish. Be a cobbler.

By the time I return to camp, about ten minutes later, Alan and Sunny are still sitting there talking and laughing. Richard and Stewart are conferring in the kitchen about the night's meal, and Marv has talked Pete into a glass of whiskey and a game of backgammon. As they play, the third member of Sunny's crew wanders up into camp. She introduces him as Gary, and as she goes around the group, ticking off our names, I'm impressed to see that she has remembered every one.

"I just checked the sleeping bags," he announces to Sunny and Pete as he takes a seat. "Still a little damp." He looks up at the sun, which is about to disappear behind the canyon wall. "I don't know, could be a cold night."

"Well, we've got whiskey to fend off the chills if it comes to that," I offer. "Can I make you one on the rocks?"

"You have ice? Out here? How do you manage that?"

I smile at him.

"Well, we've done this before. We've got a few tricks."

Over at the backgammon board, Marv has won his game against Pete. He starts rearranging the pieces, setting up for a new game, and he's talking up a storm.

"Backgammon is like life, Pete. It is a game of skill, in which you must manage the odds to your benefit. It is cruel but honest, cruel but honest."

"Jesus, Marv, where did you get that shit? Quit acting like an asshole," says Alan. "We have guests."

"You wanna try me, A-Book?" says Marv, a big grin on his face. "I want my money back. C'mon. Your luck has run out."

You can tell that Alan is reluctant to leave his seat next to Sunny.

They seem to have something cooking. But he's also eager to play. Finally she nudges his elbow, gesturing toward Marv.

"Go ahead," she says. "I'll watch. I used to play a lot in college."

"All right," Alan says. "Somebody around here needs a lesson in humility anyway."

"Oh yes, oh yes," says Marv, rattling his dice in anticipation as Alan slides into the spot where Pete had been. "The ferret is my inspiration, inflicting death on all opponents. Come, sit down beside me, Mr. Alan the Squirrel."

The Big Swede takes a big swig of whiskey, and they begin.

The early rolls go Marv's way, which only fuels his motormouth. He doubles the bet, and Alan calmly accepts. Everybody in camp has now circled around the board, which is propped up between the two competitors on a little camp stool. Even Richard has walked over from the stove to watch.

"That ferret . . . he's probably down in that hole sleeping right now, with a big belly full of squirrel meat," says Marv. "There are predators in this world, and there are prey. You're one or the other. The thrill of the kill."

He splashes the dice onto the board with a theatrical flourish.

Alan just sits there quietly, a grim little smile on his face as he studies the board. I know my brother, and at the moment he doesn't look much like a squirrel to me.

Marv studies his options. He can attack or play conservatively, but to Marv that's no choice at all. He attacks but misses, leaving himself vulnerable. Alan picks up the dice and rolls a six and a four, a perfect counterattack. Two of Marv's pieces come off the board. With one roll, the advantage has changed dramatically.

Now it's Alan's turn to double the bet. Marv has a choice—he can accept the redoubled bet or concede the game. But with all his talk, he cannot let himself back down.

"Damn. You are so lucky," he tells Alan, accepting the double.

Now Alan's conservative play really begins to pay dividends. Marv is stuck. Alan rolls, moves. Marv rolls, but can't get his stranded pieces back on the board.

Alan rolls, double sixes. Best roll possible. The rout is on. By the end of the game, Marv finds himself gammoned, which doubles the bet yet again. It's another $6.50 on his tab to Alan.

"I can't believe you are so damn lucky," Marv says again as he gets up from the chair.

"What's that you were saying, Marv?" says Alan. " 'Backgammon is like life, Pete? A game of skill, cruel but honest'?"

Now Marv is mad. He marches over to his pack of cigarettes, muttering. Then he turns around to face Alan.

"You! You are . . . *invisible* to me!"

And that just sets the four of us to roaring.

At first, Sunny and her friends don't know what to make of Marv's snit fit. But once they see the rest of us rolling on the ground, they join in the laughter.

Marv stands there in the middle of the camp, still fuming a bit. He pulls a cigarette from the pack, puts it to his mouth, and lights it.

"I feel like that stupid squirrel," he finally says, a pained smirk on his face.

And the campsite erupts again.

A few minutes later, I notice Marv digging down deep into one of the coolers. He emerges holding two clear plastic bags, one in each hand.

"Gentlemen—and gentle lady—Richard and I have a treat for you. A little appetizer for us all, barbecued ribs that I cooked up back home."

Then Richard pulls out his own surprise: a brand-new miniature propane-fired gas grill, about eighteen inches long and eight inches wide, still in its box. He gets his new contraption fired up, and about ten minutes later Marv is serving deliciously crunchy reheated ribs to an appreciative crowd.

"I just have one question," Stewie says as he gnaws happily on a rib, barbecue sauce staining his fingers and face. "How did you hide these things all this time? I thought I knew all the food we had in these coolers."

Marv just smiles.

"Know your enemy, Stew, know your enemy. I may suck at backgammon, but when it comes to food, I know better than to let you find it."

Dinner that night is spectacular. Fresh-caught native trout are a delicacy, and in Richard's hands they reach their full potential. More whiskey bottles come out of backpacks, and Gary pulls out a little illicit smoke, which he somehow managed to keep dry. Those who still partake, partake. We hear the story of our guests' misadventures in Whitehorse, and much to my friends' delight, I'm forced by the crowd to recount my own humiliation as well.

Eventually, Sunny announces that she's headed back to camp, and we all bid her good night. A little while later, Marv notices that someone else is missing as well, that "ferret-faced Bookman brother," as he puts it.

"He's still here, Marv," Richard says. "He's just invisible to you, remember?"

But Alan, it seems, has indeed melted away into the night without saying a word.

"Boy, when you make someone invisible, you do a damn good job," Gary says to Marv.

"I had nothing to do with it. Personally, I suspect your friend Sunny might be involved."

In Sunny's absence, we interrogate Gary and Pete about their friend, and they do the same about Alan. No, I tell them, Alan has never been married, and he split with his last girlfriend about six months ago.

Gary and Pete, it turns out, have known Sunny since junior high school, near the town of Salem, where they all grew up; and no, she doesn't have a boyfriend. She now works for the state of Oregon, in the Department of Environmental Quality.

An hour or so later, just when the stories have petered out and we're about to call it a night, Alan emerges from the darkness as wordlessly as he had vanished.

"Where'd you go?" Richard asks.

"Just for a walk, upstream away from you loud assholes," Alan says, his smile suggesting that any further information would not be forthcoming.

A few minutes later, everyone has retired to bed for the night. Gary and Pete are gone. Stewie, Marv, and Richard have disappeared into their tents, zipping them up behind them. Alan and I lie on the tarp, staring up at the sky in our nightly ritual, watching for shooting stars. Finally, my fraternal curiosity takes over.

"So. Sunny seems nice."

"Yes, she is. She's . . . I like her style. She says she might even be coming down to Austin soon. I guess she has some friends there she wants to visit. She's really sharp. She works for the state, a biologist."

"I know. And she's from Salem."

"Huh." He falls silent for a moment. "I take it you guys were exchanging information with Gary and Pete?"

"Little bit. Got to watch out for my baby brother, you know? You two were gone a long time. It made you the natural topic of conversation."

"Yeah, well, don't mention this to Mom or she'll be wondering where her wedding invitation is."

"Okay," I chuckle, because I know he's exactly right. "Good night."

Sometime later, I'm awakened by the rumble of a train chugging up the canyon, straining under a heavy load. The train is still downstream, well out of sight, but as I sit up in my sleeping bag I can see the beam from the locomotive's powerful front lamp ricocheting off the canyon walls as the train twists and turns up the grade, creating a dramatic shifting of shadows and light. A minute later the locomotive itself comes into view, lit up like an alien spaceship, throwing its beam against canyon walls a mile upstream from us. Behind it come clattering boxcars and flatbeds loaded with wheat, wood pulp, lumber, and other raw materials. After the last car passes in front of us along the opposite bank and then disappears behind a bend, headed to California by morning, I lie back in my bag and stare up at the stars.

"Don't you think there's something lonely in the sound of a train disappearing into the distance," I say softly to Boose. "It's as if it's going off and leaving you behind."

Alan makes no response. I turn to see if he's managed to sleep through it all, but he's nowhere to be found. His air mattress and other gear are still here, but wherever he's gone to, he has taken his sleeping bag with him.

day five

I lie there on my side, my head propped in my hand, watching in the early-morning dimness as the water comes crashing down through the last of Whitehorse, as it had all night and all day and all night and day before that for time immemorial, always full of anger and relentless, incessant power.

Then it pours that fury into the deep, accepting peace of the downstream eddy. Even there, the river's unspent energy plays out in roiling, sucking whirlpools that seem to dance inside the water.

Lulled back toward peace, I surrender, consenting to a few more minutes of sweet sleep. . . .

Holy shit.

Something's there, right behind me. I can hear it rustling on the tarp, just a few feet away. My eyes fly open, but I lie still, afraid to move, almost afraid to breathe.

My mind races through the possibilities. Skunk? Raccoon? Maybe even a coyote?

What do I do? Damn, there it is again. And I'm helpless. Even my arms are trapped down inside this sleeping bag.

Slowly, so I don't startle whatever it is, I shift position so I can pull my arms out of the bag. Once free, I stop again to listen. Nothing. But it's still right there, I know it is. It hasn't moved away. I shift my weight again and slowly, very slowly, my arms up to protect my face, I roll over to see . . .

. . . Alan, calmly sitting up in his sleeping bag, getting ready to light his morning Marlboro, as though he had spent all night there and it's just the start of another day on the river.

"Morning, bro," he says, flicking his lighter and then drawing deep on his cigarette. Damn I wish he'd break that habit. One of these years he, or Marv, or Richard, isn't going to make the trip because he let that tobacco kill him.

"Sleep okay?" he says, exhaling a lungful of smoke.

I nod as I struggle to sit up.

"That train wake you up last night?" he finally asks, staring out over the water. "I thought it was pretty damn cool coming up the canyon."

"Um, I don't know," I tell him, playing along. "I think maybe I remember hearing it. But I slept pretty sound. Must have been that whiskey last night."

"Yeah. Must have been."

He picks up a rock about the size of a quarter and tosses it at Marv's tent.

"C'mon, you damn Republicans. Time to get out of bed. It's moving day."

And out of the tent comes Marv's voice.

"Once again you liberals are no doubt sitting on your asses, waiting till somebody productive wakes up to do your work for you."

Unbelievable. The guy wakes up thinking this stuff.

"You know, Marv," I finally say, "I know a lot of good, reasonable people who are conservatives. You just aren't one of them."

"Screw you, man."

I pull on my shorts and a shirt and walk down to the calmer part of the river. The day feels like a hot one already. The sky is cloudless, and there's no morning chill in the air. As I walk I realize with surprise how good I feel; most of the stiffness and soreness is gone. I think it was all that time floating yesterday. It was like taking a full-body ice-cold whirlpool. Still, I'm going to take a couple of aspirin first chance I get.

I glance upstream at Camp Sunny. Their two tents are a couple of hundred yards from us, but from this distance there's no sign of movement. The clothes they had scattered out on the sagebrush yesterday are still there, no doubt bone-dry by now. There's no morning dew in the desert.

I look over to see Alan wandering down to join me at the riverbank.

"Marv and Richard are up," he reports. "Stewie's still sacked out."

"I guess we should let him sleep, huh? We really don't have far to go today. If we camp right below Buckskin, that's only about ten miles."

Alan nods. We stand there, watching the pink dawn of the sky reflected in the dark, swirling water. Then I notice Alan's head jerk. Sunny has emerged from the nearer of the two tents. She starts picking clothing items off the brush, one by one. Once she has an armload, she crawls back inside the tent.

She does look beautiful.

I'm just about to broach the subject when Alan, saying nothing, turns and walks back up toward the kitchen area, where Richard is already puttering around, getting the coffee going.

Over the next couple of hours, we grab a quick breakfast of instant oatmeal, coffee, and orange juice, then break camp. The tents come down, the tarp is folded, the sleeping bags are rolled up and tucked away in the waterproof river bags. Once all our personal gear is packed away, we start dismantling the kitchen. By the time the sun comes over the canyon wall, our boats are once again piled high with gear; the main coolers have been restocked with ice, lunches, beer, and bottled water; and the final pieces of equipment, the lounge chairs, have been strapped into place.

It always astounds me, how empty the campsite looks once we've packed away all our gear. One minute it's full of human activity, with stuff strewn everywhere; the next it's as if we had never been here.

Sunny, Pete, and Gary have wandered down to see us off. Richard gives them a couple of spare containers of propane for their stove, which should be enough to get them through the rest of their trip.

They're going to hang around the camp for a while, to make sure their craft is seaworthy and to let their stuff finish drying. According to Gary and Pete, their sleeping bags were still a little damp last night.

Sunny is silent on the subject of sleeping bags.

If things work out, they may break camp by early afternoon, which means we could still see them again downriver. Like us, they've got only two more days to float the remaining thirty miles, so they'd like to move at least a little farther downstream today.

Sunny steps up to give each of us a hug good-bye, and when she gets to Alan I watch their body language carefully. Pete, I notice, also seems curious. But they play it cool, giving nothing away.

Then it's into the boats and off we go. I'm riding with Stewart again; Richard's with Marv, and Alan is strapping on his life jacket. He has the kayak today. He had reserved it for this stretch of river before we even left the launch site three days ago. He's headed a few miles downstream, to a fishing spot we call Bookman Bend, named in Alan's honor. He discovered it on one of our first trips, more than a decade ago, and it's probably the sweetest hole on the river. With the kayak he can get there early, before anybody else has a chance to fish it.

I get settled at the oars and signal to Stewie to shove us off. After a whole day as a landlubber it's good to feel the river underneath us again, to hear the sounds, breathe in the smell of fresh, clean water. I spin us around so we're facing downstream. Ten miles of river ahead.

"So, where do you want to go first?" I ask.

"I was thinking about trying that spot right down here, on the other side of the railroad tunnel. Marv and Richard said they did pretty well there yesterday."

"Okay. Sounds good."

I get us positioned in the middle of the current, then let the river push us along. The early-morning promise of a hot day has already been kept. It's not close to noon yet, and it's probably a hundred degrees out here already. I pull a red paisley bandanna out of my cargo shorts and dip it into the cold water, getting it good and soaked. Then I drape it over my head, and pull my Red Sox cap down tight to hold it in place.

The water trickles down my neck, chest, and back, and I shiver briefly. It really cools you down, but you have to repeat the process every fifteen minutes or so because the bandanna dries out quickly.

I feel the current picking up speed beneath us as we slide into the first little rapid. Stewart has turned to face me, his back to the river. He's hunched over tying a lure to his fishing line, so he's not paying attention to where we're headed.

Oh, what the hell.

I casually study the rapid ahead, looking for the biggest wave I can find. Then I aim the raft right at it, nose first. Stewie is still bent over, intent on his knot, oblivious of what's about to happen to him.

Careful, right on line, now just let it glide. . . .

Perfect. As we dip and then hit the wave head-on, cold water comes splashing up over the front of the raft, soaking Stewart's back. He flinches as if somebody has just stuck him with a cattle prod.

"You son of a bitch! Bastard. Ohhh, that feels goooood."

I always get a chuckle out of doing that.

Once we get downriver a little bit, we can see tents ahead on the right, near where we were hoping to fish. Sure enough, as we draw closer, someone is standing out on the point, fishing line in the water.

We wave as we float by. The canyon gets more narrow after this, and the river picks up speed. It'll be another mile or two now before there's another good fishing spot.

Up ahead, a black steel train trestle crosses the river. It's a historic spot. Almost a hundred years ago, this canyon was the site of the last great railroad war of the American West. From 1908 to 1911, two barons of the railroad industry, James J. Hill of the Northern Pacific and Edward H. Harriman of the Union Pacific and Southern Pacific, raced to build a line from the lush Columbia Valley up this canyon, and then out onto the high plains above us.

Their immediate goal was access to the timber and sheep industries of central Oregon, which needed a way to get their goods to market. From there, though, Hill intended to extend his line farther south to San Francisco, where the real money could be made. That would give him a link between California and the Northwest and allow him to compete with Harriman, who at the time had a monopoly on freight between the two regions.

And Harriman, wanting to protect his lucrative market, was equally intent on stopping his rival.

So for three years, two crews of more than a thousand men each, one on the east bank, one on the west bank, fought nature and each other as they blasted tunnels into the rock, carved railbeds into the canyon wall, and laid track through this harsh desert climate.

Historical accounts of the contest make it seem less a race than a movable brawl, fought with fists, guns, explosives, and lawyers. In one episode set down in railway legend, one of Harriman's work crews came across a large mass of writhing, intertwined rattlesnakes, looking something like a ball of living rope. If the description sounds too bizarre to be true, I can vouch for its accuracy. I've seen a similar thing myself on a hike: a round, heaving mass of garter snakes that was at least a foot in diameter.

Biologists call the phenomenon a mating ball. It's a rite of spring, occurring right after the snakes emerge from winter hibernation. They're cold-blooded animals, and the friction among so many writhing bodies apparently helps get their body temperature up. If you can imagine a snake orgy, you've got some idea what it looks like.

As the story goes, Harriman's crew captured the still-sluggish rattlers and sealed them into burlap bags. That night, they smuggled their booty across the river to Hill's construction camp, opened the bags among the sleeping workmen, and scampered back to their own side of the river.

When first light came, Hill's workmen—most of them Italian immigrants—found their campsite infested with rattlesnakes. That proved the last straw for some of them. They hightailed it out of camp, out of the canyon, and out of the story.

Right here, at this spot where the trestle crosses overhead from the left bank to the right, the war finally came to its head. Harriman had succeeded in buying up enough property to block Hill's route farther upriver, leaving him nowhere to go. So, after intervention by the federal government, the two sides negotiated a compromise: Hill would be allowed to share use of the eastern track for the next eleven miles so he could complete his line into central Oregon. In return, he had to abandon plans to extend his line south into California.

We pass beneath the trestle, avoiding a large uprooted tree in the middle of the channel. From here the river broadens and slows again, making it more suitable for fishing. The left side is still reservation land, so I maneuver us to float along the right bank so we can pull over quickly if we see a likely spot.

Stewart, still sitting at the front of the boat, gestures silently up into the sky behind me. I turn to look. Buzzards, eight of them, are floating in single file on the air currents a couple hundred feet above us. From down here they appear as magnificent black silhouettes floating against a deep blue backdrop, each of them stretching six feet from wing tip to wing tip.

As we watch, two of the birds peel off from the line, one to the left and one to the right. Each performs a series of slow, tight little wheeling maneuvers before falling back into formation. Then another two birds peel away and begin to make tight little circles of their own. They look as though they're pirouetting on their wing tips.

They're flying a search pattern, working together to spot carrion. But from down here it looks like something far more elegant, like a choreographed dance sequence in one of those old Busby Berkeley musicals.

All of a sudden we bang against the rocks lining the right bank.

"Shit," I say, grabbing at the oars to pull us away from shore. "Sorry, Stew, got distracted."

"No problem," he says, still staring up at the birds. Once I get us back under control and away from the bank, I glance over my shoulder again. But the show's over; they've disappeared over a ridgeline.

I turn my attention back downstream.

"Well, you ready to pull over and do some fishing?"

"Definitely. How about right up there, where that rock is sticking out."

"Okay, get ready to jump out and tie us up."

As we beach the raft, Marv and Richard come floating up behind us, waving silently as they pass. Alan, in the kayak, is already well ahead, probably casting a line into Bookman Bend by now.

After we tie the raft to the shoreline—you have to make sure it's secure, because you don't want to look up and see your raft floating downstream without you—I trudge upstream about a hundred yards while Stewart heads downstream. The current is moving at a perfect pace through here, steady but not too fast. It's good holding water for fish, and the trees along the bank provide shade for fish and fishermen alike.

Sure enough, I catch and release three nice fish in about fifteen minutes, one of them a beautiful sixteen-incher. By the time I fish the hole out and make my way back to the boat, Stewart has returned. He's sitting on the cooler, happily gnawing on a barbecued rib.

"Where the hell did you get those?" I ask, astonished. "I thought we ate 'em all last night."

"Ah, Mr. Bookman," he says with a smirk on his sauce-smeared face. "You will find that there are certain advantages to traveling with Stewart."

He reaches behind him and pulls out a plastic bag filled with ribs. "Want one?"

"You'd make a helluva buzzard, Stewie. You're the best scavenger I ever saw."

The ribs do taste good, though.

About a half hour later we float by Alan, Marv, and Richard, all of them fishing at Bookman Bend. It's a long, sweeping curve, about a quarter mile of good fishing water, so there's plenty of room for all three of them.

Alan stands at the top of the run, where the biggest fish would be holding. As we float by we see him smile and hold his hands about two feet apart. Then he flashes three fingers our way. Three big fish already in that spot.

"Sorry, no more room here," Marv yells across the water as we pass the lower part of the hole. "All taken. Caught two here so far, more to come."

"That's okay," Stew yells back, holding up the bag of ribs. "We're just having lunch."

I have rarely seen Marv left speechless, but there he is, a stunned look on his face. By the time he manages to get words coming out of his mouth, we've floated so far past him that the sound of the upcoming rapid almost drowns out whatever he's yelling. But over the noise we can just make out the words:

"Rib-stealing bastards!"

Once we're through the white water and back into calm water, I reach down and wet my bandanna again. It's well past noon by now, and the heat has begun to get ridiculous. The wind has picked up, hot and dry, and there's no shade out here in the middle of the river, but to tell you the truth, I don't want any today. I'm a human lizard—I just want to sit here and soak it up. The sun is so intense that it's like a drug. It alters your state of consciousness.

As with any drug, though, you've got to get your dosage right. You've got to watch yourself. You let the sun bake you into a stupor for a while, then use the ice-cold river to smack you back into awareness.

I notice movement on the railroad bed along the left bank, and point it out to Stewart. It's our friends the buzzards, come down to earth. They've found the mangled carcass of a white-tailed deer that had been hit by a train, probably the train that passed through last night. Now that I think about it, the buzzards probably cruise up and down that rail line, day after day, looking for fresh kills just like this.

We stare silently at the scene as we pass. A couple of the buzzards look up from their feast and return the stare, red dripping from their bills.

After about a half hour of floating we rouse ourselves long enough to pull over and fish again. The wind is really beginning to pick up now, as it often does on hot days like this. It can easily gust up to fifty miles per hour through this canyon, making it difficult to fish or even handle the boat.

I catch a few, but by this stage of the trip just catching fish has become mundane; I'm prowling for something big, something in the eighteen-to-twenty-inch range.

As I look up, I see Marv and Richard come floating by.

"We're heading on into camp," Richard yells, "before this wind gets any worse!"

I nod. There's no sign of Alan. He must be staying a while longer back at Bookman Bend. I reel my line in and splash through the shallows back to the bank. I'm ready to make camp too. The sun is one thing, but in just the past few minutes the wind has gotten even worse. And it's no fun getting your face and body sandblasted by twenty-five-mile-per-hour wind.

By the time I get back to where we beached the boat, Stewart's there again, this time with the line untied and ready to push off. He's done for the day as well.

Once out on the water, though, we find it hard to make headway. These large inflatable rafts aren't exactly designed to slice gracefully through a gale, and the wind blowing up the canyon has stopped us dead in our tracks.

"Time to throw out the bucket, Stew."

Each boat comes equipped with a large plastic bailing bucket. A few years ago, we discovered that if you tie the bucket to the front of the raft, then toss it overboard, the bucket sinks beneath the surface and acts like an underwater sail. The current grabs it, then pulls the bucket and raft downstream, right through the wind.

"Yeah, good idea," he says.

Stew's not very handy with the oars—that's why I do most of the rowing. But as a kid growing up in Connecticut he did a lot of sailing, and he can tie you a sheepshank knot slick as can be. In just a few minutes, the bucket has been deployed and we're back under full steam, moving about three miles per hour even through the wind.

All we can do is sit back and bake in the sun, hunkering down out of the wind as we let the bucket do its work.

I lean back against the stack of equipment and take in the sights, letting my mind go blank. Stewie stretches out on the wooden bench at the front of the boat, a life jacket serving as a pillow, staring up into the sky.

It's perfectly quiet, except for the slap of the water against the boat and the whistle of the breeze. It's blowing so hard that the fishing lines on our rods have begun to vibrate and sing.

My wife once asked me what we talk about out here when we're floating downriver. When I told her that we rarely say much, she laughed out loud.

"Well, you can bet it would be a lot different if there were girls on that trip," she said.

A couple of years later, Marv and I did bring our families out here for a week, just to satisfy their curiosity about what it was like. We all had a great time, and the trip generated some favorite family stories. The next year we did it again. But it turned out that the sun, the water, the gentle rocking of the boat, and the stark scenery are all gender neutral. They have the same hypnotic effect on women as on men.

"I see what you mean about this place," Julie told me at one point, after about an hour of silence. I just smiled from behind my sunglasses and said nothing.

Silence can be awkward in the real world. We treat it as a vacuum that must be filled, if not by conversation then by music or the blaring of the television set or the car radio. I don't know why silence should feel so natural out here and so artificial elsewhere. But it does.

I give a half pull to the left oar to keep us in the deep water.

Until now, we've been surveying the countryside from a lofty perspective, like those buzzards circling high overhead. Maybe it's time to come down to earth for a little bit, to talk about technology's impact in more practical terms.

For the most part, we have to accept that the larger world—the world beyond our immediate grasp—isn't going to make much sense. Partly by design, partly by accident, it has become much more chaotic and difficult to understand. It simply will not have a story line that we can follow, and those who claim to understand it all should be viewed with deep suspicion.

But on a more personal level, we seek the same goals that human beings have always sought, the security and happiness of ourselves and our loved ones, and a sense of meaning garnered from trying to achieve those goals. But sometimes our tools interfere.

Take television. As we've seen, with hundreds of cable channels available, each devoted to serving a very thin slice of the American demographic, TV now has the capacity to fragment the communal even at its fundamental unit, the household. You can even argue that with the remote control, which allows a solitary person to flip at will among the channels and watch three or four shows at once, TV can fragment the individual as well.

How do you confront and manage that challenge? Barring TV altogether is not an option, at least not for me. It plays too big a part in the man-made world we occupy; refusing to partake of TV can be as socially isolating as giving in to it entirely.

We can, however, use television in ways that minimize its fragmenting power. Take them out of individual bedrooms, and keep them only in common areas in the household. Make it a point to turn on only one TV at a time. Such ground rules encourage family members to share television time, to share interests, to watch the same shows and to compromise in show selection. A potentially isolating technology can become a source of unity.

Personally, the fact that I've sat and watched TV with our two daughters as they've grown up has greatly enriched my life. I can, for example, tell Chucky from Tommy on the *Rugrats* cartoon, although those darned Olson twins still have me bamboozled. It wasn't exactly the programming I would have selected if I had been sitting there by myself, but given the company I was keeping, it was enjoyable.

Conversely, having sat by my side through more than a few baseball games, my daughters now know a 6-4-3 double play when they see one.

If we don't take such steps—if our children are allowed or even encouraged to draw information not from the communal well but from the pipes laid directly to their own bedrooms—then we as parents abandon our roles as molders of our children, ceding that power instead to the media outlets that supply them with information.

Cell phones pose a similar management challenge. Doing without one is possible, but why? It's a great little device, useful in so many ways. The problem develops when the cell phone or Black-Berry becomes such an integral part of you that the idea of leaving it behind is appalling. The concept that you must have a cell phone with you at all times in case someone needs to reach you is equal parts egotism and insecurity.

As a rule, none of us is that important. The world can get along without you. And believe it or not, you can get along without the world. Leave the cell phone at home sometimes—make yourself inaccessible to anybody but yourself and those you're with, if not for a week on the river then for just an hour or two. Cut down on the distractions that fragment your sense of time and self.

"People try to get away from it all—to the country, to the beach, to the mountains," a wise man once observed to himself. "You always wish that you could too. Which is idiotic: You can get away from it anytime you like.

"By going within."

The man in question was Marcus Aurelius, the second-century Roman emperor, writing in a book of personal meditations. Even back then, Marcus Aurelius recognized the importance of making time for himself. And if he could do it, so can you. Busy as you might be, you're not running the Roman Empire.

Sometimes even those who do get away "to the country, to the beach, to the mountains" end up bringing the world and its addictive distractions with them. I've never seen anyone using a cell phone on the river, but that's only because they can't get a call through from down in this canyon. I've certainly seen people at the beach, standing knee-deep in water, staring out at the beautiful horizon while they discuss business with someone back at the office. You've seen it too, or something much like it. Maybe you've even been that person.

There's an absurd contradiction, a negation, between the two activities. It's like seeing an obese person on a treadmill, trying desperately to lose weight while simultaneously scarfing down a pint of Häagen-Dazs.

In fact, I think there's a strong parallel between obesity and technological addiction. In our hunter-gatherer past, when we humans had to scrounge for any food we could get, our bodies evolved to crave ripe fruit, which was sweet and full of sugar, and animal fat, which was rich in calories, minerals, and vitamins. In some of us, such as Stewart, the legacy of that distant past remains particularly powerful.

But that adaptive trait, so valuable to a hunter-gatherer, has become maladaptive in a modern world in which sweets and fats are so readily available. Because we were molded by a world of scarcity, we aren't genetically prepared for a world of plenty. As a consequence, obesity has become the largest health problem confronting Americans today, outranking tobacco, alcohol, and other drugs. We have yet to learn, individually or as a culture, how to overcome the instructions that our genes keep sending us.

We have also become obese in terms of information and communication, and for much the same reason. As with sweets and fats, we have been genetically programmed to crave information, communication, novelty. We don't know how to say no to it, and in fact don't want to. We have yet to evolve the tools, the cultural norms and ideologies, that would help us overcome our genetic maladaption.

As a consequence, we have built a culture that is enamored of the new, fascinated by the new, addicted to the new. We constantly consume new, from those five hundred cable channels and those twenty-four-hour news broadcasts. New doesn't even have to be important; it need only be new. New trumps important every time.

We use new to sell things—more clothes to those with closets already overflowing, more kitchen appliances to those already too busy to cook, more electronics to people already buzzing and beeping. Affluent consumers already own one or two of everything conceivable; so they don't need stuff, they need new stuff.

It is, as they say, a New Economy, a term more profound than most people understand.

The human imagination used to be enough to satisfy our taste for new. It showed us new ways of looking at the world, new ways of understanding ourselves and each other. But as our taste for new became an addiction, as new became the fuel that drove the economy, our imagination faltered under the burden. It couldn't meet demand. The human imagination is still a pure, clear spring of new, but what we require these days is a raging river.

So what do we do?

Well, we distill new from the old. We sample or remix old songs to make new songs. We plunder fifty years of television and a century of cinema. We remake old movies, make sequels to old movies, re-create old movies line for line and call them new. ESPN Classic shows old football games, old boxing matches. And you know the ransacking of our cultural closet is all but complete when Hollywood is down to redoing *George of the Jungle* and *Dudley Do-Right*.

And oh yeah, Roller Derby and studio wrestling. It may be old to you, but it's new to someone out there.

But what do we do when we've run out of past, when the old made new becomes old again?

Like vampires, we suck the new out of our children.

Kids look at the world fresh, taking it apart and putting it back together in new combinations. It's always been a joy to see the world through the eyes of a child.

But now that joy is bought, packaged, and sold. Corporations hire scouts to prowl nightclubs, streets, schools, Internet sites, trying to pick up the barest scent of something new and track it down to its source. Because these days, if you can deliver new, or even the illusion of new, they'll make you a director, a producer, an Internet king.

But kids produce new for a reason. They need it to define themselves, to mark themselves as different from their parents, to create a world and identity of their own. So if we adults steal and commodify everything they invent, nothing new is theirs for long. In their desperation to find someplace we won't invade, some trend we won't co-opt, they turn to facial tattoos and nipple rings, slamdancing and violent fantasies too often made real.

Anybody want to follow them there?

No? Well, maybe tomorrow.

The richest lode of new lies in forbidden territory, those thoughts and ideas off-limits for hundreds if not thousands of years, things that cultural taboos and simple good taste once prohibited. Deviance and crudity and cruelty, aspects of our humanity that we long ago concluded were better off left private if not buried, have become our most profitable source of new.

That territory used to be the domain of the artist, who would mix small doses of the forbidden with bits of his own imagination and use the result to educate, to force us to think and see things from a new perspective. Artists were professional children, creating the new and driven by instinct and vision to live on the fringes, at the boundary between the acceptable and the unacceptable.

But now that we've commodified the forbidden, now that we've enlisted the profit motive to exploit and deliver the forbidden to a mass audience, there's little room left for the artist. To go where mere commerce dare not follow, the would-be artist is reduced to dipping a crucifix in urine or depicting the Madonna through the medium of elephant dung.

Even forbidden territory, though, turns out to be a finite resource of new. I mean, once you've seen Michael Jackson's face and read about Bill Clinton and his cigar, what else is left?

It's interesting to speculate how we found ourselves in this predicament. Maybe it's because as our world has broadened, it has also grown more shallow. New is what makes that world possible; it is the coin of the realm, the currency of our superficial conversation.

"Have you heard . . . ?"

"Did you see . . . ?"

"Have you tried . . . ?"

"Have you been to . . . ?"

And the velocity of new—the time it takes for new to become old—is accelerating. Like any addict, we must consume more and more new to get our high. And we're running out. Our kids are tapped out, our artists are desperate, and the past is all but wrung dry.

But still we want more. More, more, give us more.

I give the left oar another touch.

"You got a cold beer in that cooler, Jay?" says Stewie, munching on another rib. "I'm getting thirsty."

The cooler doubles as my rowing bench, so I have to stand to get at the beer. I lift the lid and pull out two cold cans, and hand one to Stewart. The second one I crack open and pour down my gullet. I can feel the coldness travel all the way down into my gut.

I look downstream.

"Okay, Stew, we're coming up on some rapids, time to pull the bucket up."

"Yeah, okay, let me finish this," Stew says, gnawing on the last rib. The now empty bag lies on the boat floor.

I pull back on the oars, trying to slow us down a bit in the accelerating current to give Stewart a little more time, but the bucket is stronger than I am. The water's getting shallow quickly. I look over the side; I can see the rocks on the bottom.

"You better hurry, it's coming up fast. Stewart? Stewart!"

He takes another leisurely bite from the rib and finally sits up, looking downstream at the looming rapids.

Crunch. The bucket hits bottom and is pinned between the rocks and the boat. The handle breaks free under the strain, and as I peer over the side of the raft I see the white bucket floating away beneath us, no longer attached to the rope, gone.

I look up at my raftmate. He looks back at me and shrugs, takes a last bite from the rib, and returns to his prone position.

So there are also disadvantages to riding with Stewart.

Once we're through that little rapid, we come to another long stretch of slow water. The wind is still howling in our face, and now our bucket is gone. For his sins, I make Stewart row us through this section while I take his lounging spot. I feel my back and legs stiffening, a lingering legacy of my misadventure two days ago.

Fortunately, what Stew lacks in rowing technique he makes up for with brute strength, and a little while later I see the landmark warning of Buckskin Mary ahead. We make the sharp left turn, and sure enough, even in the wind you can hear the roar of the rapid about a half mile ahead.

"Well, you want to take us through, Stew?"

"Sure," he says. "I've done this one before."

We both reach for our life jackets.

As rapids go, Buckskin offers a good ride, but it's nothing very difficult or technical. The river is funneled through a narrow gorge here, and it drops quickly in elevation, so as the water rushes through the gorge it buckles up to form a series of four standing waves, each about six- to eight-feet high.

You just point the nose of the raft at the middle of the rapid, keep the thing straight, and hold on for the roller-coaster ride.

Stewie sets us up perfectly and guides us through the waves. I get totally soaked, but man, it's a great ride. And the cold water feels great on my skin.

We float a little farther, about another quarter mile, and pull off to the right—our camp spot for the night. Marv and Richard are already there. They've unloaded their boat and are sitting in the shade, waiting for us.

About an hour later, Stew and I have unloaded our gear as well, and the four of us are laughing and talking quietly. There's still no sign of Alan. I'd be worried, except that he doesn't have to negotiate any serious white water between here and Bookman Bend. A little while later, Richard points out a patch of bright red through the trees, headed down the river our way. It's the kayak, moving toward camp.

I get out of my chair and stroll down to the water, but to my surprise it's Gary at the paddle.

"Alan said you guys would be right here," he says, a little breathless and dripping wet, as I grab the front of his kayak and pull him toward shore. "Boy, fighting that wind is a bitch!"

"Is Alan all right?"

"Oh yeah, definitely. He's on the big boat. He was fishing upstream when we came by, and he offered to let me try this thing. It's a blast, dude. Right up there, in that white water? I lost it big time. It flipped me right out. What do you call that rapid, with all those waves?"

"Buckskin Mary."

"Yeah. Buckin' Mary. It's a good name for it."

I don't bother to correct him, because he's right: "Buckin' Mary"—I like it.

"C'mon up, we'll get you a beer."

It's fun walking into the circle with Gary. Richard and Stewie are clearly surprised to see him. Marv, though, seems to have expected it all along.

"Alan riding with Sunny, I gather?" he says.

"Uh, yeah. He should be here pretty soon," says Gary.

"Good. I want my revenge at backgammon. Grab yourself a beer outta the cooler and have a seat. I was just telling the guys about this big fish I nailed today."

An hour later, Alan, Sunny, and Pete finally show up, pulling into the vacant campsite just downstream from us. Richard and I walk down to meet them.

"I am so hot," says Pete as he splashes ashore. "I'm dying."

"I see Gary made it down all right," Alan says from the boat as he throws me the bow rope. He gestures upstream to the kayak, now sitting up on the bank, out of the water.

"Yeah, it was a bit of a surprise to see him, but he made it, yeah. We were getting a little worried about you, bro."

"What can I say, a better ride came along."

"So I see," I say, tying the boat to one of the trees lining the bank.

As the five of us walk up to the campsite, Pete steps alongside me.

"Hey, Alan and Sunny were telling us about doing—what'd you call it, Alan?—a Buckskin Marv? Do you guys really do that?"

"Sure. We're about ready to go. You game?"

"Oh yeah. I'm so hot, I was getting fried out there in the sun. And it sounds like a blast."

"Cool. Get your life jacket. One for Gary too."

"And one for me," Sunny says. I feel sheepish. I should have known she'd be game for it.

Gary, it turns out, is a bit dubious about the idea of floating through "Buckin' Mary" wearing only a life jacket. Sunny's coming, though, so Gary doesn't dare to back out. The only nonparticipant is Richard. In all the years we've done this, he has never floated the rapids. Something about his bad back, he says. He also thinks we're a little nuts, and maybe that's true as well.

In a few minutes all eight of us are marching along the old rail bed, headed back upstream. When we reach Buckskin, Richard stops at a large rock overlooking the rapid.

"Here," says Sunny, handing him a little throwaway camera.

"Take some shots as we come through here. My dad hasn't been out here in years, and he'd love to see photos of us doing this."

The rest of us hike on a couple of hundred yards farther. It's incredibly hot up on the rail bed, away from the water, with the canyon wall radiating heat at you. It's like walking through a reflector oven. By the time we reach the steep trail leading down to the river, our tongues are hanging out and I'm about ready to dive into the cold water.

We make our way down to the bank and then regroup at the water's edge, snapping tight our life jackets, retying our river shoes. Marv gives last-minute instructions to Gary and Pete, who have looks of real concern on their faces. I don't blame them. I remember the first time I did it.

"Okay, any wimps in the crowd need to leave now," Marv says, raising his voice above the roar of the white water. "Once you're in the water, you're committed. Everybody good to go?"

Six heads bob up and down.

"All right, here's what we do then. We swim out right here, go as straight across as the current will let you. Then you form up in a single line behind me. It's real easy. All you do is aim for that V, right at the bottom of the V. Don't go to either side or you'll get pushed into the rocks and it'll mess you up. Then, when you get through the white water, start swimming hard to the right bank until we're sure that everybody has made it. Got it?"

Pete and Gary nod their heads. Alan and I smile.

Marv takes a couple of steps deeper into the river, then dives in headfirst and starts swimming hard toward the middle of the channel, with Sunny right behind him.

"You guys gonna do this?" I ask Gary and Pete, and they both nod one more time. So I dive in after Sunny and then turn to wave them in. Gary comes next, then Stewie, Pete, and finally Alan, ever the caboose.

Almost immediately, I can feel the power of the current grab me.

It's a bit intimidating because I no longer have control over my own body. I take a full crawl stroke and a hard kick, and move about a foot sideways and about ten feet downstream.

I look behind me. Everybody's set, all lined up. Ahead of us, Marv and Sunny are about forty feet away. I see Marv hit the top of the rapid, give a loud whoop, then disappear from view as he's sucked down the chute. A few seconds later Sunny does the same, her arms held high in the sky as if she's headed down a roller coaster.

"Oh man, I can't do this! I'm going back," I hear Gary say behind me.

Shit. I look back. He's starting to dog-paddle for shore. I'm too far ahead of him and the current has me. I can't do a thing to stop him. Thank God Stewart's right there.

"*No!*" I hear Stew yell, and he reaches out and grabs Gary's life jacket in his paw. "It's too late! The river will slam you into those rocks! Stay in line!"

Gary complies.

Crisis averted, I turn forward again and kick my way about a foot farther left, so I'm set up to hit the V perfectly. The current is really ripping now. You're just a piece of driftwood at this point. Once in position I glance behind me one more time. Good. Gary is in line, but he looks as though he's living out his worst nightmare. There's sheer terror on his face.

I chuckle to myself. He hasn't even hit the scary part yet.

Here I go.

I hit the crest of the white water, and for a millisecond everything seems to pause. I get a peek at the rapid for the first time, and those waves down there look enormous.

Then I'm sucked into the V, like a hairball into a vacuum cleaner.

Slap! I get smashed into a mountain of water. I have no control whatsoever now, and while I'm underwater I feel a momentary panic, a flashback to Whitehorse.

I come out of the first wave, take a gulp of air, and *slap!*—the second one slams me. I bob back up to the surface, riding down the back of the wave, enjoying it now, only to get smacked by the third, then the fourth.

And then it's over. I'm in the calm water, exhilarated. I spin to look back, and there's Gary, coming out of the last wave. He spits water and takes a big gulp of air, then sees me watching.

Big grin, two thumbs up. He liked it, or at least claims to. I tread water, fighting the current, kicking over toward the slower water on the right bank where Marv and Sunny are already floating, waiting for us.

"Oh man. I'm not even cold anymore," Gary finally says, breathless and excited. "That was incredible! I can't believe I did that. Oh man. Where's Pete? Is he through yet?"

Stew comes floating over, and he and I exchange raised eyebrows. Gary doesn't know how close he came to killing himself. Pete clears the last rapid, with Alan right behind. They start paddling toward the slack water, where we're waiting. Once Pete's out of the current, he floats over to Gary and they high-five.

Then, once everyone's calmed down a little from the excitement, the seven of us push off again for the quarter-mile float back to camp, our life jackets a little looser now for comfort through the slower water. Gary and Pete chatter all the way down, still giddy. Alan and Sunny float a few yards apart from the rest of us, not saying anything that the rest of us can hear. By the time we reach land, slogging up out of the water to camp, our legs numb and stumbling from the cold, Richard is waiting for us.

It's evening now, and the sun is still shining directly down on the campsite. The wind is still blowing too, and it's well over 110 degrees. But it won't be for long.

For the last few miles the canyon has gotten gradually tighter. Now the rock walls loom two thousand feet above us, leaving just a narrow window of sky. The sun has begun to edge behind the western cliffs, and in another fifteen minutes it will disappear altogether, leaving us in shadows for the rest of the evening.

It's time to get out of these wet shorts and into some dry clothes. It's amazing how good it feels, at the end of a day on the water, to put on a pair of jeans, a fresh T-shirt, some clean, dry socks, and a pair of good, solid shoes. All the others are doing the same, I notice, rifling through packs, organizing their personal space for the evening. Sunny and her crew are over at their boat, pulling tents and other gear off. The whole campsite is buzzing with activity, yet it's also strangely quiet, with everyone engrossed in his own business, preparing for the fall of evening.

Once I'm dressed, I grab a bottle of Gatorade from a cooler, then pull my chair out of the shade and into the day's last remnants of direct sunlight. I want to let my body soak up some heat after the chill of the water, and before the cool of the coming darkness. I face south, away from the gusting wind, looking back up the canyon where we came from.

With everything quiet for the moment, this is a good opportunity to finish what we had started earlier. As Thomas Hobbes put it, "Leisure is the mother of philosophy," and who am I to argue?

I think I mentioned that eliminating television from your life probably isn't wise, given the dominant role it plays in our culture. To bar yourself from television is to bar yourself from the mainstream, to condemn yourself to the fringes.

The same has become true of e-mail. Back in the mid-eighties, only the early adopters even knew e-mail existed, and the only people they could e-mail were other people like themselves. As more people were drawn to the medium, though, it grew more useful and attractive. By the late nineties, tens of millions of people had acquired e-mail accounts and were using them daily.

Economists would explain the rapid adoption of e-mail by citing the network effect. It works like this:

An e-mail system is a network, and according to Metcalfe's law—technophiles do have a penchant for formulating "laws"—the value of any network is the square of the number of people who are connected to it. The law is named after Bob Metcalfe, an Internet pioneer.

A network of four people, then, would have a value of 4×4, or 16 . . . well, there are no standard units of network value, so let's call it 16 Metcalfes. A network of eight people would then have a value of 64 Metcalfes, and a network of one hundred would have a value of 10,000 Metcalfes. If a million people joined your network, it would have a value of 1 trillion Metcalfes. So you can see how quickly a network's value can increase as people join.

The value of a network can also be expressed as the cost of choosing *not* to join. In the example of e-mail, by the late nineties the network had become so large—and membership so valuable—that the price of rejecting the technology had grown prohibitive. In many circles, so much social and business information was being transmitted by e-mail that opting to stay out of the system was tantamount to opting out of society and business altogether. Even the hard-core Luddites had to give in. Among those under thirty, the concept of not connecting is considered all but absurd.

The fast expansion of the cell phone network has followed a similar path. Not long ago, only crazy people would be walking down the street talking loudly to themselves, or standing in the grocery store holding what appeared to be a serious conversation with the tomatoes in the produce department. But today, for growing numbers of people, a hands-free cell phone has become something like a watch or a pair of eyeglasses, just another piece of equipment that they don each morning and wear all day long. As that equipment becomes less obtrusive, and as the network effect kicks in, it seems inevitable that someday we'll all be fruit-talkers.

Given that history, it's interesting to anticipate how the network effect might play out from here. Ultimately, the goal of the communications industry will be to make every person in the world accessible to every other person twenty-four hours a day, seven days a week, via text, voice, and image. It's not a far-fetched ambition. In some parts of the country, some demographic groups have pretty much attained that goal through a combination of cell phones, beepers, Palm Pilots, and BlackBerries. The objective now is to meld those devices into one small multipurpose unit.

Consider the example of Steve Mann, a professor at the University of Toronto, the same place where Marshall McLuhan developed and taught his insights into modern mass media.

Mann is a self-described cyborg, a melding of man and machine. In all his waking hours, he wears what appears to be a pair of very dark sunglasses. In reality, they act more like a blindfold, blocking all outside light from reaching his eyes.

But Mann can still see what's going on around him.

Two small electronic cameras—one mounted on each side of Mann's glasses—transmit images via a closed-circuit wireless network to the Internet. From there, the signals are retransmitted to laser devices that are mounted inside Mann's glasses.

Those devices project video images directly onto Mann's retinas. Mann doesn't see a thing of the world around him; he sees a streaming computer video of that world. And if he wants to mount a camera pointed behind him, he could almost literally give himself an eye in the back of his head.

Mann's eyesight is perfectly normal, and he uses this wearable computer by choice. In fact, when he was still a student at MIT, Mann would post the video feed from his glasses live on a public Internet site and allow visitors to see his daily life as he experienced it, in real time. Through that Internet connection, they could even send e-mails to Mann that, like the images, would be projected on his retinas.

"For two years, I had thirty thousand people inside my head, watching what I did every day, altering my reality, offering suggestions on what I should do next," he told me in a phone conversation. "I finally had to shut it down, though. My head space got a little too crowded."

While it operated, the system gave Mann almost superhuman powers, because the people watching on the Internet could participate in his world.

"I could recognize people I had never met, recognize buildings I'd never seen," Mann recalled. "If I was in a store, somebody [on the Internet] might tell me, 'Hey, I went to high school with that clerk right there,' and then he'd tell me her name."

Mann now restricts access to his Internet feed to people such as his wife, Betty. Among other things, it allows Betty to look over her husband's shoulder when he's out food shopping.

"If I'm at the milk counter, she can use her computer to draw a glowing circle around the low-fat carton, guiding me away from the full-fat variety," Mann said.

For the moment, the computer that Mann wears is still too primitive and cumbersome to win broad public acceptance. Furthermore, most people may never want the full suite of equipment that he carries. But in the future, as computing power continues to miniaturize and as batteries become more lightweight, people in our highly competitive, hyperconnected world will almost certainly embrace some form of a truly wearable "personal computer" encapsulating e-mail, cell phone, wireless Internet connection, and database. All that will become "standard equipment" for a twenty-first-century adult. Those who might want to resist will once again be confronted with the choice of joining the network or dropping out.

But if that happens, if we do become a tightly connected network of computerized cyborgs, then at least this particular trend will have played itself out, right?

Well, maybe not.

Scientists are also making stunning progress in forging direct physical links between computers and the brain. For example, they have succeeded in growing brain cells on top of computer chips so that the living neurons intertwine with the circuits. They have attached an electronic probe to the brains of monkeys, allowing the monkeys to manipulate a computer cursor with their thoughts and play a crude video game. They have conducted similar trials using human subjects who by virtue of disease or accident have been completely paralyzed. Electrodes attached directly into their skull allow them to operate a computer through mind control. Researchers at UCLA are even designing tiny computer chips that mimic the operation of human neurons, intending the chips to be implanted in the human brain to replace damaged tissue, or perhaps even to artificially augment healthy brains.

Kasparov, in other words, could eventually find himself across a chessboard from someone whose intelligence and memory have been increased with an electronic brain implant. Human creativity directly connected to brute processing power would be a formidable opponent.

Kevin Warwick, a professor at the University of Reading in England, has already had an electronic chip surgically implanted in his arm and then connected to his central nervous system. The chip can send and receive wireless signals, directly connecting Warwick's body to a computer.

And Warwick, like Mann, describes himself as a cyborg.

"As we link up more and more closely with technology," Warwick told me, "we will see a conflict between those who are human and those who have become superhuman. Some of us will have extra senses, a superior ability to communicate, access to far greater processing power, the ability to think part machine, part human. Your power will come with being a node in a computer network rather than as the individual that you are."

That vision has also been embraced by one of the most famous scientists of our era, British physicist Stephen Hawking. Hawking is physically incapacitated by disease; his brain now serves as the onboard command center for his wheelchair, his voice synthesizer, and other equipment. But while the necessity of such a system is obvious in Hawking's case, he believes a direct brain-computer link will eventually be necessary for healthy people as well.

Like others who have dared to look twenty years into the future, Hawking sees a very real danger that our machines will become more powerful and intelligent than we are, and he's concerned about how to meet that challenge.

"With genetic engineering, we will be able to increase the complexity of our DNA, and improve the human race," he told a German magazine. "But it will be a slow process, because one will have to wait about 18 years to see the effect of changes to the genetic code. By contrast, computers double their speed and memories every 18 months. There is a real danger that computers will develop intelligence and take over. We urgently need to develop direct connections to the brain, so that computers can add to human intelligence, rather than be in opposition."

Most people—not all, certainly, but most—would be far less comfortable with the prospects outlined by Mann, Warwick, and Hawking than those three seem to be. If we were to take a vote on whether to pursue that vision as the future of mankind, it would be defeated overwhelmingly.

But no vote will ever be taken. The future is not subject to democratic decision making. To the contrary, there seems to be something inexorable about the progression from cell phone to chip-implanted cyborg. Each step seems to lead naturally to the next, then the next. If there are obstacles to implementing that vision of mankind's future, they are probably more technical than social. If we can do it, we probably will.

But why is such an outcome inevitable, especially when it contradicts the wishes of most people on the planet? Has technology truly slipped the control of its creators, to pursue a fate of its own and sweep us along behind it?

No. As always, technology does what we tell it to do. But it responds to what we really want, not what we merely claim to want, or think we want, or are supposed to want. That has always been its value, and its danger.

For example, we claim to want technology to liberate us from labor. That's been the excuse from the very beginning. The earliest expression I can find of that sentiment comes from a Greek poet from the first century B.C., Antipater of Thessalonica. In a passage that invoked both Demeter, the goddess of the harvest, and the Nymphs, the guardians of water, Antipater gushed like some high-tech stock tout about the merits of the newly invented grain mill, which used water power to turn the stones that ground wheat into flour:

> Cease from grinding, ye women who toil at the mill; sleep late even if the crowing cocks announce the dawn. For Demeter has ordered the Nymphs to perform the work of your hands, and they, leaping down on the top of the wheel, turn its axle which, with its revolving spokes, turns the heavy concave Nisyrian millstones. We taste again the joys of the primitive life, learning to feast on the products of Demeter without labor.

To me, the most fascinating phrase of that passage comes in the last sentence, "We taste again the joys of the primitive life." Even in the first century B.C., people were harkening still further back, nostalgic even then for some mythical era of primordial purity.

But somehow I don't believe that things worked out as Antipater anticipated. While the invention of the water mill might have saved the slave women from their literal "daily grind," I expect that the next day, they still had to rise with the crowing cocks and go to work.

The reason is obvious: The real goal of the water mill was never to let slave women sleep later. The ancient Greeks wanted the mill to make those women more productive, to let them grind more grain than ever in their twelve- or fourteen-hour day. Then as now, we may wax rhapsodic about the labor-saving power of technology, but in truth we rarely use it to create free time, for ourselves or anyone else. Instead, we reinvest that saved time into some other activity, hoping to increase our productivity still further.

For the Greeks, and for people throughout most of human history, that was a wise reinvestment, over time producing an ever higher standard of living. You do have to wonder, though, when the law of diminishing returns kicks in. Here in the United States, as the level of consumption soared through the latter half of the twentieth century, the level of happiness reflected in polls and surveys actually declined. Beyond a certain income level—a level that undoubtedly varies from individual to individual—additional income purchased at the cost of additional stress and time away from family and friends would seem a bad deal.

Most of us don't need scientific surveys or polls to tell us that; we know it intuitively, based on our own personal lives and the lives of those around us. And yet for some reason, it's difficult to act on that knowledge.

Already harried and overscheduled, we use personal computers and the Internet to smuggle still more work into our home life. Cell phones purchased to make life less hectic have the opposite impact. Laptops are marketed as providers of freedom, yet in practice they become ways to take work with us on the road, in airports and hotel rooms. I'm particularly fascinated by the conflicting messages within TV commercials that show someone pounding away on a laptop while she sits on a porch with beautiful mountain scenery in the background, or at a beach house overlooking the crashing surf. The unspoken but apparently widely shared assumption is that this is somehow a good thing.

If we hope to understand why we employ technology as we do, if we seek to be something other than its passive subjects, we need to look not at the technology but at ourselves. Our technology is responding to something powerful but unconscious, some metaphor or ideology whose impact we do not yet fully comprehend.

"Hey, J-Book, Planet Earth calling. You look way too serious, dude."

I look up to see Marv, standing in front of me like a tall, anxious five-year-old waiting for his mother to take him somewhere.

"I need a victim, a Bookman victim," he says. "C'mon. I've got the board set up right over there."

"Don't you want Alan instead? Or is he still invisible to you?"

"Might as well be," he says, nodding his head to his left. I follow his glance. There are Alan and Sunny, sitting off by themselves talking. They seem to be dropping any pretense, which I guess is just as well. They weren't fooling anybody anyway.

Then we hear it, all of us. The sound seems to come rolling in from everywhere at once. Heads begin to swivel, eyes scanning up and down the river, trying to locate the source. It's a low, ominous rumble, echoing up through the canyon.

"Train?" I say.

"Thunderstorm," says Marv.

Eight heads turn up toward the sliver of sky above us. It's absolutely clear, not a cloud in sight.

"Somewhere down the canyon, I bet. It's echoing off the walls up to here."

Just as he says that the wind—still roaring up the canyon—drops in temperature about fifteen degrees, and with the coolness comes a sense of moisture as well. Another rumble is heard, this one closer and sharper.

That's the damn thing about being down in this part of the canyon. You can't see any weather coming. There might be a hellacious thunderstorm headed our way right now, but our little window on the world is too narrow to let us see it coming. All we can know is the present, and that looks deceivingly harmless.

But the other signs . . . the signs are not good.

"Hey, Jay, what do we do?" Stewie says.

"We get busy," I respond.

The laid-back atmosphere disappears. Sunny, Gary, and Pete hustle back to their boat to make sure everything is storm-ready. Richard grabs Stewie, and together they run down to our two rafts, to make sure they're tied up well and everything's protected from the rain. Alan and I grab our small emergency tent. In ten years on the river we've slept every night out on the tarp, underneath a cloudless, starry sky. Tonight, that streak may end.

I stretch out the musty tent and pound stakes into the desert hardpan while Alan assembles the poles. While we work, one eye on the sky, Richard and Stewart walk over, ready for another chore.

"You guys mind if we take your tarp, since you won't be using it?" Richard asks. "We're gonna string it up between those trees over there, to make a shelter."

Another roll of thunder, this one closer still.

"Sure, I guess so," I say.

"Okay, great. We'll bring your sleeping bags over," Richard says as they hustle off to where the tarp sits, piled with our gear.

"Well, that settles that," I say to Alan as we finish setting up the tent. "I guess we're sleeping Republican tonight. Hope it's not too crowded in this thing."

"Oh, I think you might be sleeping alone tonight anyway," he says, giving me a funny look. "Hope you won't get scared, in the storm and all."

"No, I'll be fine," I tell him, giving him a funny look of my own. "I'm getting used to it. Little brother's finally leaving home."

Another rumble echoes off the canyon walls.

"It's coming from the north," says Marv, splashing his way out of the water and back up the bank into camp. "You can see it from out in the river now. Black clouds. Lightning too. It's gonna hit us in just a few minutes."

Stewie shows up with our sleeping bags. We toss them inside the tent.

"Get the rest of my gear in there, will you?" Alan asks. "I'm gonna go see if those other guys need any help."

"Such a humanitarian."

A few minutes later, all of us have stowed our personal gear away and are helping to tie down the large tarp in a wind that's intensifying quickly. From our campsite, we can see the storm coming upriver like a black blanket being pulled up over the canyon.

The tarp is about thirty feet long and ten feet wide, made of sturdy green plastic, so once it's up it ought to provide good shelter. But it's awkward to handle in this wind. Tall Marv, teetering on a cooler, ties off two corners to high tree branches. Stewie and I pound stakes into the ground, then tie off the other two corners.

We stand back. We've created a large lean-to, its open side to the south, away from the storm. The tarp catches the wind, then bows inward, like a sail. I hope the stakes hold.

A pulse of light illuminates the canyon walls around us, as if a flashbulb has just gone off.

Then a loud crack. Heads duck, an instinctive flinch.

We all look to the sky to see black strands of rain advancing up the canyon. Sunny, Pete, Gary, and Alan scamper up from the other campsite, their arms full of gear.

While the rest of us stare in awe at what's coming, Richard starts pulling the stove and chairs under our new shelter. There's another flash of light and another loud crack.

"Jesus. Look!"

Stewie points to a high peak on the opposite side of the canyon. That last lightning strike has left a charred black circle on the hillside, and smoke is starting to rise from the parched grass.

"Oh man," says Marv, staring at the spot. "We better hope the rain puts that out, or we could be in trouble."

"A fire couldn't jump the river to our side, could it?"

"No, but the smoke would. And we could get a lightning fire on this side just as easy."

Now you can hear the rain coming. You can even smell it.

I poke my head outside the shelter to watch it advance. Upstream the river is hissing and boiling under the hard rain. Fat, heavy drops slap the leaves of the trees above us and hit the ground so hard that they kick up little dust balls, and leave little craters in the dry desert floor. Then little balls of hail start coming down, bouncing off the ground.

The rain smashes into the tarp and sweeps over us like a wave. The sound fills the air, and the tarp, which once seemed so big, now feels puny and inadequate.

I look around. No one's smiling. Sunny and Alan are standing close together, not quite touching. Stew has rustled up a bag of Fritos.

Craaaccckkk!

No time at all passes between the flash of light and the sudden earsplitting noise. The sound rumbles through the canyon, bouncing from side to side for thirty seconds or more.

"Well, I think we're safe from the lightning," I say. "It probably won't hit this low. But I sure wouldn't want to be up on that plateau right now."

"And I don't think we have to worry about fire anymore," says Gary, holding his arm out into the rain for a moment. When he pulls it back it's soaking wet. We all giggle, the tension relieved for a moment.

"How about a flash flood?" says Sunny, loud enough to be heard above the constant thrumming of the rain.

The gloom redescends. That particular danger hadn't crossed my mind yet. A few of us move to the left side of the shelter, up toward the canyon walls, studying the terrain to try to figure out where the water might flow.

"Whose is that?" Sunny asks, pointing to a distinctive green-and-yellow tent, the colors of the University of Oregon Fighting Ducks, Marv's alma mater.

"It's mine," Marv says. "And I see why you ask."

So can I. Marv has chosen a nice, soft sandy area to pitch his tent, great for sleeping no doubt. But peering through the pelting rain, we see that the sand has been washed there over the years by storms just like this one. And "upstream" of his tent, we can discern the outlines of a dry gully feeding right to his location. In fact, a trickle of water is already making its way through the rocks about twenty feet up the slight incline. If it keeps up like this, he's gonna be in trouble.

Bang!

The lightning hits again, and again we all jump. Then it echoes for a long time before it is drowned out by the pelting of the rain-drops. At least the hail has stopped.

But that worrisome little trickle is gaining volume.

Marv, staring at his predicament, makes a decision.

"I have to go get it. If it gets flooded out, I'm doomed. I'm gonna move it over there to the right, out of the wash."

Alan and I volunteer to help, and a quick division of labor is decided upon. Alan and I will pull the stakes. Marv will grab the top of the tent, where the poles meet, and together we'll move it to higher ground. It should take only a few minutes, tops. There's just one problem.

"Man, I don't want to get these dry clothes soaked," I say. "It's the only pair of long pants and warm shirt that I brought."

"Me too," says Alan.

We stare out at the rain again, all of us now huddled against the back of the tarp, where the splash of falling water can't get us. Our other clothes are in the tent, and none of us has bothered to bring rain gear.

Sunny starts laughing.

"Well, boys, I guess you're just gonna have to go out there naked."

So a few minutes later, the three of us are standing at the edge of the tarp, stripped down to our underwear, gathering courage for the mad dash into the rain. Our clothes are piled in little stacks atop a cooler. The thunder and lightning have moved down the canyon; the rumbles are getting more and more faint. The rain, however, shows no sign of letting up. If anything, it's coming down even harder. And the stream of water headed toward the tent is growing larger.

"Marv, that's one skinny ass you got there," says Stewie. "I've seen bigger cracks in my ceiling."

"Man, would you guys stop Stewie from staring at my ass," says Marv. "He's making me nervous."

"You got nothing to be nervous about. I like a little meat on my bones."

"You guys ready to go?" says Alan. "Let's get this over with."

"Okay," says Marv. "Readddyyyy . . . go!"

And out we go, into the pouring rain.

By the time we reach the tent, tiptoeing across the wet desert in our bare feet, we're soaking wet. By the time Alan and I get the stakes pulled out of the ground, we've given up trying to hurry. You can't get any wetter than wet, and the truth is, it's actually kind of fun out here.

In fact, once we get the tent relocated, the three of us stand there, grinning, letting the warm water run off our bodies in streamlets as though we were kids again, playing in the rain. Marv wipes his brow and gestures toward the tarp, beckoning the rest of them to come out and join us, but it's not necessary. Stew, Gary, and Pete are already stripping down. Richard, as usual, is having no part of this nonsense, but he does seem to enjoy the spectacle.

"Oh my God," says Marv as Stewart comes rumbling out into the rain dressed only in his underwear, a huge grin on his face.

And then, glory be, out comes Sunny. She had been wearing a long-sleeve jersey, a pair of khaki shorts, and sandals, but apparently no bra. The shorts and sandals stay on, but the jersey disappears, and she comes dancing topless from beneath the tarp, arms spread wide, face upturned to the rain, spinning and spinning. . . .

Somewhere, in the sound track of that moment, there had to be a Grateful Dead song playing.

day six

Back in the sweet days of a childhood June, summer vacations would stretch out like an endless highway that could take me anywhere I wanted to go.

I could head over to Young's field, an empty lot behind the trailer park, and play baseball all day. Or if no one was putting a game together, Alan and I might jump on our bikes and ride out to a secret pond out in the woods to go fishing.

On other days, if it was hot and the tide was coming in, I might walk to the beach and hang with our summer friends, the kids from Boston who migrated down to our little Cape Cod town each Memorial Day and stayed through Labor Day. All in all, if time was riches—and it was, and is—I was a rich little boy. I couldn't make a wrong decision—what I didn't do today, I could always try tomorrow.

But each year, as June and July passed and we moved into August, fall would start to loom larger on the calendar. Each day of freedom became sweeter, more precious. I gradually became conscious that my choices had consequences, that deciding to play ball today might mean I was forfeiting my last chance to go bike riding that summer. It was one of the hardest parts of growing up, the realization that by opening one door you had to close off many others, sometimes permanently.

So you know where I'm going with this. Today will be our last day on the river, and I'm feeling a little melancholy.

From this point on, the opportunities for fishing—and for solitude—will be slim. We have about twenty river miles to cover today, which works out to about a third of the total distance we travel on this trip. It'll go pretty quickly because the stretch includes some of the fastest, most exciting white water on the Deschutes, a series of class 3 and 4 rapids—Wapinitia, Boxcar, Oak Springs, and White River—in quick succession.

That part's a blast.

We'll have company, though. A public road begins about five miles downstream from here, and once we hit that point the character of the river changes dramatically. The road brings up daytrippers, car campers, and white-water rafting tours by the busload. That's why we always stay at this site on the final night; it's one of the last good camping spots still unreachable by the motoring public.

Downstream, the river will be crowded with all kinds of people: church youth groups in flotillas of three or four rafts, each with half a dozen fresh-faced paddlers under the supervision of a professional rafting guide; groups of loud, obnoxious drunk teenagers who treat that part of the river as an aquatic bumper-car ride; large tour groups from Japan or China, a little awed by the scenery and a little intimidated by the raucous party atmosphere.

In some years we've looked downstream on a long, straight stretch to see forty or fifty boats clogging up the river, most of them engaged in horseplay and water fights. Richard calls it "the splash-and-giggle crowd."

For the most part, though, even the rowdiest groups steer wide of our little crew. They tend to be dressed in brightly colored bathing suits, all clean and cute and bright-eyed from their showers that morning in Portland or Bend or Beaverton. The five of us come float-ing out of the mountains looking a little different—dirty, unshaved, sunburned and grizzled, our boats stacked high with well-worn camping gear and plastic trash bags filled with empty beer cans. Even the meticulous Richard could pass for a homeless person on any city street in America. So some of the stares we get are pretty funny.

We probably return the stares. After days of quiet and solitude, the sight of all those people is not exactly welcome. Usually, I love the excitement and buzz of a big city; people watching is one of my favorite pastimes. But spending time on the river turns me into a temporary misanthrope. It has taught me how the old-time fur trap-pers must have felt when they came down out of the mountains and back into civilization. The scene just seems unnecessarily . . . intense.

At the moment, though, I'm sitting on the riverbank about half a mile upstream from camp, fishing pole idle by my side, staring out at the landscape and listening to the river gurgle. It's early. Before anybody else was stirring, I crawled out of my tent and trudged up here, just to spend some time alone.

To my right, the sun still dawdles beneath the eastern horizon, as if it too is reluctant to see the day begin. It paints the morning sky in a palette of pastel blue, pink, yellow, and violet, colors picked up in the swirling river as well.

A few clouds still linger overhead, the remnants of last night's storm. The rain went on for several hours, and huddled in my dry, warm sleeping bag, I was serenaded to sleep by the pleasant thump-ing of raindrops on canvas.

This morning, the rain has seemed to bring everything into sharper focus. The green of the trees along the river seems more vibrant; everything's had a good scrubbing. The desert soil, usually a light tan, is dark from the moisture.

The skies at this hour are still empty; the ospreys, swallows, and kingfishers have yet to make an appearance. I've caught the desert in a shift change. The night crew is headed home, and the daytime workers haven't punched in.

Looking around, just taking in the stillness, I finally spot a patch of white moving through the trees and sagebrush along the opposite bank. It's a coyote, a large and healthy one, probably coming home after a night of hunting.

It trots forward a few paces, stares nervously around, trots a few paces more, and stops again, sniffing the air. The wind is coming from my back, so the cool morning breeze is probably carrying my man scent across the river. But as the coyote scans the bank where I sit quietly, hidden among the trees, its gaze passes right over me.

It knows I'm over here somewhere, but as long as I don't move, it can't find me.

It trots a few more yards—an elegant, almost prancing step, more refined than that of a toy poodle at the Westminster Dog Show—then stops and turns once again to stare in my general direction, its nose twitching.

I stare back, still motionless. It's not often that you get to watch a wild animal like this. Usually, I'm sure, it's the other way around. They watch us all the time, and we're not even aware of it.

Until Lewis and Clark ran across the coyote in 1804, nobody in the eastern United States even knew this animal existed. Now it has adapted so well to its changing environment that you can find coyotes just about anywhere in the country, from the western prairies to the suburbs of New York City and Boston. This guy right here is a coyote from the old school, making a living—and a pretty good one from the looks of him—the traditional way.

Native Americans in the West have long admired the coyote's cleverness and adaptability, and in fact enshrined him as a central figure in their mythology for just that reason. One story recounts how Coyote stole fire from the sun and gave it to mankind. Another gives Coyote credit for creating salmon. Many tribes, including those of the Northwest, saw Coyote as a shape-shifter, able to assume whatever form was necessary to take advantage of a situation.

As things turned out, they weren't far wrong.

Finally, maybe spooked by its inability to spot me, the coyote moves away from the river, glancing over its shoulder in my general direction as it trots into a ravine and disappears.

I stand up, stretch my limbs, and pick up my fishing pole. It's time to get a line in the water, even if it's still a little early for much action.

I draw my wrist back and flick the lure directly across from me, toward the opposite bank where the coyote had been, then watch as the line swings downstream in the current. Waiting, waiting for the hit . . . not this time.

I begin the retrieve—slowly, because sometimes you get a take as the lure comes back in. Then I cast out again, this time farther out into the current.

We humans, of course, aren't bad at shape-shifting ourselves. We may not be able to change our physical form, as the mythological Coyote could, but we can and do change how we think of ourselves. And by changing how we think of ourselves, we change how we function, and we assume new powers. That's our unique gift as a species.

Historically, we have always tried to emulate what we most admired, embracing as our model whatever we deemed to be most powerful.

When God still sat unchallenged on his throne, we humans told ourselves that we had been created in his image, and we organized ourselves as we believed God had organized the universe. In European culture, the top-to-bottom hierarchy of the Catholic Church, from God to angels to pope down to cardinals, bishops, and priests, with lowly sinners on the bottom rung, was reflected in a similar earthly hierarchy, from kings through nobility down to peasants. The divine right of royalty to rule here on earth was justified because it mirrored the rule of the Lord our King in heaven.

But once Isaac Newton explained the workings of the solar system with calculus and physics, a new understanding began to take hold. Since the planets seemed to orbit the sun like pieces of intricately engineered clockwork, God became the Great Clockmaker, a craftsman of intricate machines, including human beings. Our arms came to be seen as levers, our hearts as pumps, our lungs as bellows, our livers as filters.

We even began to think that if a machinist was clever enough, he might be able to duplicate God's work. It made sense: If God created life, and if we were made in God's image, then we too could create life.

Toward that end, inventors created ducks that ate and shit, mannequins that could supposedly play chess, mechanical children that could speak. Man-made life even became the theme of ballets, such as *Coppelia,* and novels, such as *Frankenstein.*

Eventually, as the machine gained power and began to transform how we lived and thought and interracted with each other, it came to usurp God's role as the central metaphor of human life. The machine became our subconscious model for how we organized ourselves, this time into precision-drilled armies, into vast national governments, into factories in which human beings were demoted from children of God to mere interchangeable pieces of something larger than themselves. If one human component broke down, it would be removed and replaced with another.

And we began to see machines everywhere.

Darwinian theory is at root a mechanical explanation for the origin of species; Freud's concept of consciousness as an interplay of the id, ego, and superego, each playing off the other, is a mechanistic construct, as is the U.S. Constitution with its vision of balancing powers among the judicial, legislative, and executive components. The concept of government as machine would reach its most chilling incarnation in Nazi Germany, the Stalinist Soviet Union, and

Mao's China, all of which used it as a tool to attempt social engineering on a vast and ultimately tragic scale.

By the late twentieth century, though, the machine had itself been usurped by the computer as the dominant metaphor. Information—data—was now perceived as the stuff of which the world is made, and physical reality was nothing more than information made tangible. DNA was data that expressed itself in physical form so it could sustain itself from generation to generation. Our brains—once imagined as a meshing of gears—were now understood as a collection of electronic circuits. Businesses were urged to think of themselves not as machines that cranked out goods, but as collectors and manipulators of information. The universe itself was perceived as a massive general-purpose computer, crunching information and executing the formulas and algorithms of its initial programming to produce the world we see around us.

"Beneath all the complex phenomena we see in physics there lies some simple program, which, if run for long enough, would reproduce our universe in every detail," computer scientist Stephen Wolfram asserts in his 1,192-page tome, *A New Kind of Science.*

Standing here on this rock, watching the river flow by and letting my thoughts wander where they will, it is difficult to believe that all this is somehow preordained by a mathematical formula: God the Master Clockmaker replaced by God the Master Programmer. Besides, in that concept of an original program controlling all lurks a grim cyber-Calvinism that I cannot accept.

High up on the canyon walls, now, the first bit of sunshine appears, sheathing the black volcanic rock in gold. . . . No, I can't believe that a program produces this.

Lately, though, even the computer as metaphor has lost some of its luster. For all its power to transform, it has been superseded in our imagination by something more powerful still: the Internet, the computer linked together in a network. The Net has given us a new and exciting way of explaining what we see around us. In the era of the network, we have begun to see its presence everywhere, to embrace it as the model for all that is modern and efficient.

"Life is encoded by a complex network of molecules hidden within the cell," claims Albert-László Barabási, a physics professor at the University of Notre Dame and the author of *Linked*, a study of networks. "The Internet is a complex network of computers connected by wires. The economy is a complex network of companies, consumers, and regulatory agencies. Society is a complex network of people connected by friendship, family, and professional ties. . . .

"Society," says Barabási, "is the most familiar network to all of us. We are the nodes, and the links are our social links."

As examples of social networks in action, Barabási cites the parlor game "Six Degrees of Kevin Bacon," in which every actor in Hollywood can be linked to Bacon by six or fewer costars, or the tragic impact of Gaetan Dugas, an early HIV carrier who, in his job as an airline attendant traveling from city to city, helped to spread that disease throughout the North American gay community in the early 1980s.

Barabási's basic theme echoes that of Kevin Kelly, the founding editor of *Wired* magazine and one of the more influential voices among the "digerati," the theorists trying to work out some sense of where technology may be taking us.

"An aggregation of fragments is the only kind of whole we now have," Kelly writes. "The fragmentation of business markets, of social mores, of spiritual beliefs, of ethnicity and of truth itself into tinier and tinier shards is the hallmark of this era. Our society is a working pandemonium of fragments. That's almost the definition of a distributed network."

A network is not a hierarchy, in which raw information flows up the chain of command to the decision makers, and then back down the chain of command in the form of edicts or orders to be carried out. Nor is it a highly engineered machine of specialized, regimented units, each unit performing its assigned function, as in a factory or a traditional military organization.

A network instead comprises unlimited numbers of loosely linked, highly interactive nodes, among which information flows freely and quickly, without constraints of time or distance. In a network, each node responds to the information that flows to it, and its response in turn becomes data that flow to other members of the network.

I do not doubt for a moment that we are indeed in the process of constructing a network culture. The description makes sense to me; it matches what I see around me. The rise of electronic communications has transformed each of us into an always connected node, sending and receiving data constantly, and how each of us responds to that data subtly alters the course of the world in which we live.

Politics, for example, is no longer a slow, mechanical process like that designed by our founding fathers; it is evolving rapidly toward a network model driven by the quick, simultaneous flow of information throughout the system. A talk-radio host criticizes a specific politician in his show, and within hours, thousands of complaining phone calls and e-mails swamp the politician's office. The politician responds, positively or negatively, and that response becomes fodder for the next day's talk-radio show.

Taking advantage of information technology, the U.S. military has pursued the network model as well, abandoning the traditionally rigid mechanical hierarchy in favor of a more flexible approach that pushes battlefield information and decision making down to the individual soldier. Each combatant becomes a battlefield sensor that feeds information to others within the network. The recruiting motto "An Army of One" is more than mere rhetoric; it celebrates the modern soldier's status as an increasingly independent, yet dependent, node within the system.

Capitalism too increasingly operates as a network. You make a credit card purchase, subscribe to a magazine, or register at a Web site, and that information quickly permeates the network, subtly altering how you are perceived as a consumer and what advertising is sent your way, which in turn will subtly alter what you will buy in the future.

Globalization is that same tightly bound economic network stretched across the planet, requiring the dismantling of laws and regulations that otherwise might interfere with network efficiency. Electronic mass media such as CNN also operate as a global network, connecting peoples and nations, and wireless communication does the same on a more personal level, ensuring that each of us remains plugged into the network, sending and receiving information, no matter where we go.

As Kelly describes it, "Global opinion polling in real-time 24 hours a day, seven days a week, ubiquitous telephones, asynchronous e-mail, 500 TV channels, video on demand: all these add up to the matrix for a glorious network culture, a remarkable hivelike being."

The potential importance of this change in mind-set is enormous. If Western society—once organized along mechanical lines—is indeed evolving into a "remarkable hivelike being," what are the implications?

The most obvious involves the question of control. Back when people were organized as pieces of a machine, they had to be disciplined to fill their specific roles; they had to be forced into conformity to ensure that the machine ran smoothly. Andrew Ure, an early-nineteenth-century Scottish enthusiast for the machine—in essence, the Kevin Kelly of his era—observed that the biggest challenge of the factory age then in its infancy was "in training human beings to renounce their desultory habits of work, and to identify themselves with the unvarying regularity of the complex automaton." In other words, they had to be taught to understand themselves as pieces of the machine.

Such a challenge did not discourage Ure. Quite the contrary, he and others believed that "when capital enlists science in her service, the refractory hand of labor will always be taught docility."

Or, as D. H. Lawrence described it more poetically in *The Rainbow,* human beings came to "believe that they must alter themselves to fit the pits and the place, rather than alter the pits and the place to fit themselves."

Today, those who champion the network as our new guiding metaphor celebrate the fact that the control and discipline required of a machine culture are no longer necessary. "The marvel of 'hive mind' is that no one is in control and yet an invisible hand governs, a hand that emerges from very dumb members," as Kelly asserts.

Real-life examples of that invisible hand are everywhere. The swarming of bees—none of them intelligent, none of them in control—somehow produces a beehive, an entity far more complex than any of its individual members. Our skulls enclose a network of billions of highly connected neurons, none of them in charge, but out of that chaotic tangle of cells emerges human intelligence and human consciousness.

The ecosystem of this canyon—the interaction of insects, fish, animals, birds, humans, water, sun, and wind—can be understood as a self-regulating network, as an exchange of energy and information. When it begins to get out of whack, it corrects itself.

Even the earth itself, comprising countless individual yet interconnected life-forms, is said by network enthusiasts to act as an organism of many parts, just as our bodies are composed of many cells. And like our bodies, the planet regulates itself naturally.

"Life is a networked thing—a distributed being," Kelly writes. "It is one organism extended in space and time. There is no individual life. Nowhere do we find a solo organism living. Life is always plural. . . . The apparent individuals that life has dispersed itself into are illusions."

That faith in the self-regulating power of networks draws scientific support from the work of Stuart Kauffman, a biologist and researcher into complex systems at the Santa Fe Institute in New Mexico.

In his pioneering work, Kauffman used a computer to simulate a network of hundreds of lightbulbs wired together at random. Each bulb was connected to two other bulbs, and it would turn on or off depending on what those other bulbs did.

Once the network started operating, there was no reason to expect that it would produce anything other than chaos, with lights randomly blinking on and off. No higher intelligence existed to give the system direction. Yet when Kauffman switched the network on, he discovered something intriguing. Patterns soon emerged and began to repeat themselves, as if the lightbulbs were being controlled by some outside source.

"I hope this blows your socks off," Kauffman writes in his 1994 book *At Home in the Universe.* "Mine have never recovered since I discovered this almost three decades ago. Here is, forgive me, stunning order."

It is tempting to see Kauffman's order in the lightbulbs as an illusion, as a phantom no more real than the blur of light between the bulbs reported in Wertheimer's famous experiments a century ago. But in this case I think it's real; there are too many parallels in nature to allow the phenomenon to be dismissed as a mirage.

Kauffman calls his discovery "spontaneous order," "order for free." He and others don't understand how it works; so far they can't ferret out the mathematics or laws of self-organization that might produce it. They only know that it happens, and they believe that the same type of order emerges from networks of every type. In his more visionary moments, Kauffman even suggests that this process of self-organization accounts for the creation of life itself from inanimate matter.

There's something hauntingly familiar, though, about Kauffman's assertion of order emerging naturally out of chaos. It is a refinement in scientific terms of theories that reach back almost to the beginning of the Western Enlightenment. Just as Kelly argues for the presence of an invisible hand emerging from a network, the eighteenth-century Scotsman Adam Smith, in his famous book *The Wealth of Nations,* argued that an invisible hand guides the economy, producing order and efficiency without outside intervention from government or any other party.

Applied to communication, Kauffman's work recalls the theories of John Milton and others, who argued as far back as the seventeenth century that if information was allowed to flow freely from person to person, it would in time reveal a truth that could not have been imposed from the outside. Given their eras, neither Smith nor Milton thought in terms of networks and nodes, but what they described was in many ways a network process.

All of those theories share a common thread: the claim that order emerges naturally from within the network, that attempts to impose it from the outside are almost always destructive. Kelly picks up that thread and from it weaves a claim that, having created a network culture, we are now confronted with "the dilemma that all gods must accept: that they can no longer be completely sovereign over their finest creations."

The bees, in other words, cannot try to run the beehive; they'd only screw it up. The network is smarter than we are, either individually or collectively. If we seek the productivity and efficiency it can bring us, we must give the network its head and allow it to take us where it will, trusting that in the end its decisions will be for the best.

Pierre Levy, a French cyber-*philosophe,* has his own term for the order that emerges from the network: "collective intelligence."

"Collective intelligence is less concerned with the self-control of human communities than with a fundamental *letting go* that is capable of altering our very notion of identity and the mechanisms of domination and conflict," Levy writes in his book *Collective Intelligence*. Like Kelly, he argues that while direct control was needed to make a machine system function, in a network system that control is unnecessary and even destructive.

It is tempting, then, to see the development of a network culture as the natural culmination of a long historical process. For the past five hundred years, human beings have been struggling to free themselves from the confines of each other's control. Over that time frame, we have broken the power of the church, we have broken the power of kings, we have broken the power of the tribe, of the clan, of the village, of the extended family, and now even the nuclear family, so that today the individual can rule and is ruled by only himself.

A network culture—made possible by the technology that increasingly binds us together so closely—offers us a way to advance that process further. Theoretically, a network economy no longer needs the restraining hand of government to regulate it, because it will do a better job if left to its own devices. The global economy no longer requires interference by archaic institutions such as the nation-state, and in fact trade and currency barriers only harm those they were intended to protect. Unions are no longer necessary to protect workers; they only make their members lazy and uncompetitive. Even civic clubs and political parties—mechanical units performing a function within the larger machine—are no longer necessary, because their work can be performed more quickly and directly through the Internet and television, as part of the network.

Back at the beginning of this trip, I theorized that truly influential technologies do more than merely reflect the ideology of their time. They inspire new ideologies, forcing a change in our understanding of how the world works. And on those rare occasions when a new technology and a new ideology fit together perfectly, each reinforcing the other, the pace of change accelerates and the whole culture is abruptly altered.

Well, that's what is happening now.

Our emerging network culture is the product of a synergy between network technology and network ideology. And while it is possible to have a chicken-or-egg argument about which came first—did the technology produce the ideology, or did the ideology produce the technology?—in the end it doesn't matter. They evolved together, with profound and largely unexplored implications for how we live and interact with each other.

It is futile to try to halt such a transformation—the momentum behind it is overwhelming. Besides, it's far from clear that we should even try. The potential benefits of the change are enormous, just as the benefits of the Industrial Revolution were enormous.

But even as we accept its benefits, it's critically important to try to anticipate and address the unique challenges that a network culture will pose.

For starters, while network ideology is marketed as a means to free the individual from the shackles of collective control that marked the machine age, it's important to remember that shackles come in many forms and guises.

The idea that control of the individual is eliminated or even reduced under a network system is a fraud. It merely takes another, more subtle form. The individual is no longer governed by social institutions in which he or she can exert a direct, conscious influence, but by an amorphous network that exists everywhere but nowhere, and whose signals can be disobeyed only at great cost. We have been told that modern technology gives us control over information, but the reverse is also true: In a network culture, we control information and information controls us.

Furthermore, to make the network operate smoothly, each individual node must be rendered sufficiently receptive to its messages. Any institution or idea that might make us less responsive to the network's signals, that might slow the system or insulate us from the network's power, must be eliminated. In fact, network theory and the antigovernment, hyperindividualistic political philosophy that seems so ascendant in our era are essentially the same faith in the omniscient power of the Invisible Hand, but expressed in two different jargons.

That's why so many argue today that Social Security must be privatized, that Medicare and Medicaid must be privatized, that the social safety net must be dismantled, that "government schools" must be abandoned so that individual parents can make individual choices. Those are expressions of the underlying assumption of modern American society that we must each be stripped of any collective protection to ensure that we are sufficiently responsive to the network's influence.

Insecurity, in fact, is essential to a network culture because insecurity makes it more difficult for the individual to resist the network's power. If twenty years from now we end up as the cyborgs envisioned by Mann, Hawking, and others, it will largely be a consequence of our insecurity, driving us to become things we would otherwise not wish to be. And that too will be testimony to the power of the network to enforce conformity.

The issue of insecurity is particularly significant given the nature of a network culture. Consider the network surrounding me at the moment, a more or less natural and certainly productive ecosystem. The popular notion that such systems will be stable and orderly if allowed to function naturally, without human interference, was exposed as nonsense by biologists decades ago.

This year, for example, several of us have commented that we're seeing many more ospreys than in previous years. Inevitably, that population boom of predators will create a scarcity of the smaller trout that the ospreys feed upon, leading in time to a crash of the osprey population.

So while in a rough sense and over the long term this ecosystem will indeed regulate itself, biologists have learned that it will do so by veering from one extreme to the other. Population booms and population crashes are natural and inevitable.

That may, in the long term, be the most productive way the ecosystem can operate. As Kauffman and others point out, a dynamic system such as a network is most efficient and productive when it is perched right at the edge of chaos and order. That's when new patterns, new ways of doing things, are most likely to pop up.

From the point of view of the individual osprey, though, it's far from ideal. Like a beehive or an ant colony, a network left to its own devices pays no heed whatsoever to the fate of particular individuals; they are less important than the needs of the system itself.

The stock market is another case in point. In recent years, it has evolved in ways that ought to make it a perfect test case for network ideology. More information is available these days more quickly to more people than ever before. With on-line trading, those people can act on the information more quickly as well, eliminating the stockbroker and other middlemen. The friction that once slowed the system—and according to theory, interfered in its efficient operation—has now all but disappeared.

Has the result been the "emergent order" that Kauffman's work would seem to predict?

Hardly.

Fluctuations in the market are now more severe than at any time in the market's history. Bubbles emerge, bubbles disappear, at a pace unheard of in previous boom-and-bust eras. The market has moved considerably closer to that precipice between order and chaos.

Theorists would argue that such increased volatility is acceptable if it produces more efficiency in the long term—if individual investors get crushed from time to time through no fault of their own, they will have been sacrificed for the greater good. But that tidy little theory ignores human nature. In realistic terms, if the market becomes more volatile than human investors can tolerate, they will refuse to participate, and whatever efficiencies the system might have produced will be lost.

Our tolerance for volatility is further reduced by the fact that no one can convincingly explain what particular stimulus set off the day's buying spree or selling spree. Analysts might venture that "investors today responded to rumors that the Federal Reserve might drop the discount rate by a quarter percent next month," but in reality that's just concocted to satisfy our need for story. The true workings of the network are as much a mystery to us as sunrise and sunset were to the ancient Greeks, who attributed them to Helos, driving across the sky each day in his sun chariot.

In a network culture, comprehension of what is happening is denied us. We understand how a hierarchy works; we understand a mechanical system. But Kauffman and others acknowledge that we can never understand how a network culture reaches the decisions it makes, any more than an individual bee understands how the hive operates. We are instead asked to accept the wisdom of the network as a matter of faith, and to live by its judgments.

That confusion only compounds the sense of insecurity.

The rise of network culture also raises an even more profound issue. Throughout our history, one of the prime functions of the communal has been to teach us how to live with one another. Community, in fact, has provided the foundation of our moral codes. It is not accidental that the Ten Commandments were handed down to a tribe of Israelites banished to wander for decades in the desert, reliant only on each other. As philosopher Immanuel Kant argued more than two hundred years ago, the choice of duty to others over individual self-interest is the very essence of moral conduct.

In many ways, we in the West have been living off our cultural patrimony, relying on concepts inherited from our communal past to guide our behavior as individualists. But once that tie to the communal is severed altogether, once the values and dictates of the market overwhelm those of the community in every corner of the world, what then is the source of moral conduct? Or has morality, like the communal institutions that gave it birth, simply outlived its usefulness?

I suspect that the answer to that question is no. I suspect that as we look deeper into how a network culture operates, we will find that self-interest remains a very shaky foundation on which to build a civilization, and that we will need ways to reinforce and reinvigorate moral concepts.

I look up at the sky. Helos has begun his daily journey—the sun will be peeking over the canyon rim before long. The guys back at camp are probably up by now and starting to break camp. Last cast, and then I'm heading back.

"Where the hell you been?" Marv asks as I walk into camp a little while later. "I figured you were still in your tent sleeping."

He's standing under the tarp with Stewie and Richard, waiting for a pot of coffee to start percolating.

"I wanted to get in a little early-morning fishing," I say, leaning my rod up against a large boulder, where it won't get stepped on. "Didn't even get a hit, but it was nice."

I clip the lure off the fishing line and slip it into my fanny pack, then start dismantling my rod. All eyes are on me.

"What? You're not fishing anymore?"

"I don't think so. How about you guys? You know we gotta cover a lot of river today. Won't have much time for dawdling."

"Yeah, but I'm gonna keep my rifle loaded, so to speak," Marv says. "I refuse to let the trip be over."

Stewie suddenly nods his head in the direction of the river, and we all turn to look. Here comes Alan, marching up to our site with a sleeping bag under his arm and a sheepish look on his face.

"Well, look who's making the walk of shame," Stewie says. "I never thought I'd see the day."

"Look at that expression," says Marv. "Like the cat that ate the canary. Look, I swear there's a little yellow feather sticking out of his mouth."

Alan stops about ten feet away from us and just stares.

"Any other smart-asses? I'm willing to pay the price, but let's get it out of the way right now. Anybody else got something to say?"

"Oh no no no, no matter what, it won't end here, Alan," says Richard. "You know it won't end here. It won't end this year, or next year, or even the year after that."

"I'm just shocked, Alan, that's all," says Marv. "You think you know a guy, you think you know what he's capable of, but then all of a sudden he shocks you by doing something you never would have imagined."

"What the hell are you talking about?" Alan asks, now a bit perturbed.

"I'm talking about Alan Bookman sleeping in a tent. Who would ever have thought that could happen? Next thing you know he'll be voting for George Dubya."

"C'mon, guys," Richard finally says. "I'm gonna cook up all the eggs and sausage we've got left. Stew, will you chop up those mushrooms and onions over there? And Jay and Marv, we've got dishes that still need washing from last night."

"What about Alan?" Marv asks, raising his voice to a childish whine. "Why doesn't Alan have to do anything?"

"Oh, I think Alan might need to rest up a little bit. He's looking a mite tired, don't you think?"

"Screw you guys," says Alan, still smiling. He walks over, grabs his river bag, and drags it out into the open where he can paw through it.

The others head off to their assigned duties, but my curiosity is killing me. I follow Alan. As Big Brother, old habits are hard to break. Habits like teasing Little Brother.

"So, Boose, I was thinking that when we get back to town I should call Mom, to let her know we survived another trip. But you know her—she's gonna want to book a church for the wedding. So, I need to know: What religion is Sunny, anyway?"

He doesn't even look up, just keeps stuffing his sleeping bag down into his river bag.

"I wouldn't worry about it," he finally says. "We're probably gonna elope to Vegas, but I'll make sure you get an invitation. Not going to let you off the hook for a present, you know."

"I gotta hand it to you, bro. Nobody else would ever think of the Deschutes as a hot place to pick up chicks. You have created a legend that will be recounted on many river trips to come."

"Well, we don't know how the story turns out yet," he says, finally standing up from his task and looking around the canyon. The sun is almost high enough to peek over the cliffs. "It looks as though Sunny and I are gonna come back here next month."

That makes me quiet for a moment.

"Just the two of you?"

"Just the two of us, bro."

"Damn . . . You can get the time off?"

"For this? Hell yes."

"Well. Hey, that's great. We'll talk more later, right? I gotta go wash dishes. Sunny and the others coming up? I think we have enough instant oatmeal left to feed 'em if they're in too much of a hurry to wait for breakfast."

"I'll go see in a minute. Pete and Gary hadn't come out of their tent when I left."

I wander off to find Marv, who's standing at the stove washing a plate.

"So what'd he say?"

"Who, Alan?"

"Yessss. Your baby brother. You know, the one with the ponytail and the new girlfriend?"

"He said he and Sunny are coming back out here next month."

"No shit? He's gonna fly back up from Texas?"

"And she was already planning to visit Austin in November, so they're gonna be seeing a lot of each other. Hand me that pan, will you?"

"Good luck. That stuff's baked on there." Marv grabs the pan, then holds it up in the air.

"Hey, Richard, you need this to make breakfast today?"

Richard looks over and shakes his head.

"Great," says Marv, turning back to me. "Pack it up like that and I'll clean it when we get home."

About twenty minutes later, Marv has wandered off to rummage around inside his tent, packing up. I'm sipping on a morning cup of coffee when Alan and Sunny come trudging up from the other campsite together, side by side, their shoulders bouncing off each other as they walk. It turns out that Sunny and her boys have to move out pretty quickly this morning. They're meeting their ride at 1:00 P.M. in Maupin, a little town about ten miles downriver, halfway between here and the usual takeout point. To make that deadline, they have to be on the water by a little after 9:00.

Already the clock has begun to reclaim them.

Richard has water boiling on the stove. When Pete and Gary come up, he sets out bowls, spoons, and the box of instant oatmeal. As the three of them eat, the rest of us stand around, sipping our coffee and visiting. As a courtesy, Richard has decided to wait until these guys push off before he starts our breakfast feast.

"Man, I'm pissed we're gonna have to skip Oak Springs and White River," says Gary between mouthfuls. "I hear those are good rapids."

"Probably just as well, considering how Whitehorse kicked your ass," Richard says, chuckling.

"Besides, I hear you guys are coming back out next month," says Stewie.

"Us? I wish," Gary says, shrugging it off. "I'm going to be on the road all next month for work."

Alan shoots a quick, rather annoyed look at me, and I deflect it on toward Marv, who just shakes his head. Gossip gets around quickly among these guys, even if it loses a little accuracy in the transmission.

Sunny breaks the awkward silence.

"Alan and I were talking about just the two of us bringing the raft out, last weekend in September," she says to Gary.

"Yeah, I've got some frequent flier miles that I need to use," Alan says. "And I've always wanted to see the canyon that time of year. The steelhead should be running through this section by then. I'll have to bring my gear for big fish."

The only sounds now are the rushing of the river and the scrape of spoons against empty cardboard bowls.

"It could be cold by then," Gary finally says. "It can get down to freezing that time of year."

"That'll be cool," Alan says, then pauses. "Hey, you guys need some help packing up the boat? You oughta be moving out if you're gonna reach Maupin by one."

"That's probably right," says Pete, setting down his bowl. "My brother won't like it if he has to sit there waiting for us in the parking lot."

A few minutes later, Alan and I are down at Sunny's boat, helping to pack gear. Alan's up on the boat, stowing stuff away. I'm humping equipment down from the campsite.

"Hey, Alan," says Pete, "where do you think this should go?" pointing to a river bag I just carried down. It's heavy, and appears to be cooking gear.

"Just store it somewhere low," says Alan, "so you don't get tippy going through Boxcar."

"How about here?"

"Looks good to me. Make sure it's strapped in tight."

Maybe it's just that he has more river experience than they do, but for whatever reason, Sunny's authority seems to have rubbed off on Alan. He has become her lieutenant, and it's funny to see Pete and Gary defer to his judgment.

I trudge uphill toward their campsite to see if there's anything more I can carry down. Sunny meets me coming the other way.

"We've got everything, the site's clean," she says, flashing that big smile. "Thanks. You guys are the greatest."

"Well, only one of us can be *the* greatest," I say, taking the opportunity. "And you seem to have picked him out."

"Yes I did, didn't I."

It's a statement, not a question.

"You don't think this is weird, do you?" she says. "I mean, it seems like it should be weird. Gary and Pete are acting like it's weird. But it doesn't feel that way."

I appreciate her honesty. I like blunt women.

"Well, it does look a little weird to us too. But Alan doesn't seem to think so, and that's what matters."

"Well good. Good good good. That's just great then. Thanks. Umm. There's nothing I need to know about him? He doesn't have some dark side that he's hiding?"

That makes me laugh. Blunt. Definitely blunt.

"No, no dark side that I've seen. He has a shy side, but you seem to have plowed right through that particular problem."

That smile again.

I reach for the bag she's carrying, but she pulls it away.

"Uh-uh. Now *that* would be weird. I've got it."

I follow her down the hill to the river. The sun is full on us now, and I can smell sausage and onions cooking up at our campsite. Richard got started early.

Alan and his crew are finishing up on the boat. The guys up at our site must have been keeping an eye on our progress, because they've started to filter down to the riverbank, first Marv and Stewie, then finally Richard. I don't know if they're here to say good-bye as much as to watch Alan and Sunny go through the departure ceremonies. This is a form of entertainment they could not have anticipated when the trip began, and they don't want to miss out.

Once again, there are handshakes and hugs all around. This is beginning to feel a little like déjà vu, since we went through much the same scene yesterday. When Alan finally starts heading over toward Sunny, she reaches out as if to shake hands with him, which sets off a round of snickers from the rest of us.

"Okay, you guys close your eyes, or turn around," she says, and once again everybody laughs.

"Just get it over with," Marv jokes.

"No, I mean it," Sunny says. "C'mon, just give us a moment here, will ya?"

And so we do, all six of us, turning away or averting our eyes like little boys afraid to watch a romantic movie kiss. I stare down at the ground, looking for a smooth, flat rock that I can skip across the water.

After what we saw last night, it's hard to think of Sunny as overly modest. But she already recognizes Alan's reluctance to provide a show for his buddies, and she's looking out for him. I don't know, my joke about the wedding might not be wrong, merely premature.

"All right, you guys, show's over," says Alan a moment or two later.

I sidearm the rock out onto the current—one, two, threefourfive skips, then it sinks beneath the surface.

Sunny, Gary, and Pete climb aboard and take their positions.

Then Alan and Stew push the boat free from the shallows and shove it out into the current as far as they can. Gary and Pete start digging into the water with their paddles, with Sunny on the back right side, paddling, steering, and barking out orders as they go.

We stand and watch from the bank to make sure they're safely on their way. Once they're clear, I turn to walk back up to our campsite, only to see Alan already on his way, almost twenty yards ahead of me. At the top of the bank he pauses, glances back over his shoulder one more time, then continues on alone.

A couple of hours later, we've finished breakfast and packed most of our gear. I've changed out of my jeans and into shorts, and have traded my boots for river shoes. I shove the last few things into my river bag, seal it, throw it on my shoulder, and make my way down to the boat.

It's always a little sad, breaking camp the last morning, stowing things a little more securely for the trip home on the airplane. But it feels right. . . . I'm ready.

Stew has already deflated the kayaks—the white water ahead is too much for these inflatables. Once we strap in the last bags and the chairs, we'll be ready to leave. We've also dug out our water guns— long plastic tubes with a pump mechanism that lets you shoot a stream of water about forty feet. When we reach the crowded sections down below, water fights are sure to start, and we want to be sure we've got artillery within easy reach. It's not what we come on the river for, but you do have to be able to defend yourself.

"All right, guys," says Stew once everything is packed, "time to kill the Last Soldier."

We all trudge back up to the bank overlooking the river. Stew uncorks a bottle of whiskey we had set aside last night with about three fingers' worth of Scotch remaining. He takes a swig, grimaces, and passes it down to me.

"Here's to next year," I say, taking a mouthful. Boy that stuff burns when you drink it like that. But it's become a ritual of sorts for the last morning on the river. We drink until it's finished, toss the bottle in a trash bag, then head home to civilization, where 11:00 A.M. whiskeys are not even contemplated.

I hand it on to Richard.

"And here's to Whitehorse, for kicking Jay Bookman's ass." Richard tilts his head back and lets the whiskey gurgle down his throat. My stomach flips just watching him.

Richard hands it on to Alan.

"Here's to hoping the baseball players didn't go on strike," Alan says. "Today was the deadline, wasn't it? It's Friday, right? I guess we'll find out when we get back."

"Your brother J-Book said they were going on strike for sure, and J-Book's never wrong," says Marv. "Right, J-Book?"

"If you say so, Marv."

"Yeah, but he also said there was no way George Dubya would ever be elected president," says Richard.

"That's right, he did!" Stew says. "And you know what? I don't believe he ever admitted he was wrong."

"I don't believe he ever did," says Marv, smiling at me. "I think I would have remembered if something like that had happened. But you know what? I'd start to worry if he did. A-Book gets laid and J-Book admits he was wrong, all on the same trip? One thing or the other would be weird enough, but both things happening at once would freak me out. It'd be like the world coming to an end."

Marv takes the bottle and just looks around, staring each of us in the eye, not saying a thing.

"Oh, just do it," Richard says.

"Okay, here's hoping that Mrs. Alan Bookman lets him come with us next summer."

Marv lifts the bottle up to the sky, taking the rest of the bottle straight down his gullet. Then he starts coughing and sputtering, letting loose a nonsense string of syllables, like Fred Flintstone doing his "yabba dabba doo."

We all crack up.

"You sound like you did last night when you were talking in your sleep," I tell him.

"Oh yeah?" says a suddenly worried Marv, like a big ol' trout rising to the bait. "What was I talking about, could you tell?"

"Just a bunch of words . . . random thoughts, didn't make any sense," I say. "Same as you sound when you're awake, to tell you the truth."

Another laugh, this one at Marv's expense.

Ten minutes later we're back on the rafts, floating through the first set of rapids. Alan, Richard, and I are in one boat, Stew and Marv in the other.

And once again, the landscape is changing. We're leaving the Mutton Mountains now and headed into an area marked by ancient lava flows of black basalt rock. The water moves more swiftly now, even in the long straightaways.

We're all quiet, each of us lost in thought, gazing out at the river. After about ten minutes, Marv and Stew pull to the bank to do a little fishing, but they don't stay long. A few minutes later we see them coming up behind us, rowing hard to catch up. I guess everybody's caught enough fish by now.

Every so often through this stretch, you see evidence of mankind's previous efforts to wrest a living out of this brutal landscape. An abandoned sheepherder's shack. The remains of an old ferry crossing. But the main thing that's still here is the railroad, rammed through this canyon on the backs of thousands of laborers.

The myth of the American West tells us this land was settled by rugged individualists, and to some degree that's true. It certainly wasn't a place for weaklings. But for the Native Americans who had lived here for thousands of years, as well as the later white men, working together was essential. Their network, if you want to think of it that way, was pretty tight.

To scientists, concepts of morality, ethics, and cooperation that allow us to sacrifice for each other and take risks for one another are difficult to explain. Economists have an even harder time because there's no immediate or obvious payback to cooperation and its rarer cousin, altruism.

But understanding why we cooperate is important because our ability to join together in pursuit of something larger than ourselves has been fundamental to our success as a species, and offers psychic comfort as well as practical benefits. If we are to find some way to transplant that attitude from its communal origins into a network culture, it might be helpful to know more about it.

Religions attribute that willingness to cooperate to the influence of God. There's no doubt that belief in God has, over the centuries, helped to reinforce and encourage selfless behavior, at least within each individual religious group. Between groups, religion has at times made cooperation very difficult if not impossible, but that's a topic for another day.

Instinct plays a role as well, though. When Marv thought I was in trouble at Whitehorse, he came running upriver to help. When Sunny, Gary, and Pete overturned their raft, we didn't have to offer them food and friendship. They had nothing that we needed or wanted.

Well, I shouldn't speak for Alan.

Part of the explanation may lie in the work of Robert Axelrod, a political scientist at the University of Michigan and a recipient of the MacArthur "genius" grant. Years ago, Axelrod set up a computer-simulated tournament of "agents"—software programs that act like living creatures, but in a purely digital environment. Each of Axelrod's competitors was programmed to operate by a certain set of rules—its own moral code, if you will—and then set free to mimic individuals going about the transactions of daily life.

One agent, for example, might be programmed to cooperate in every transaction with another agent. Another might be programmed to always cheat, while others were given more complex or random behavior patterns. The agents then played the game hundreds of times, over and over again, to see which strategies accumulated the most points.

Eventually, Axelrod also gave his agents the ability to evolve, like real life-forms. The least successful strategies—the approaches that accumulated the least points—were driven into extinction, while the more successful agents were allowed to "mate" with other winners, producing new combinations of potentially winning strategies.

In essence, Axelrod had created a computer world in which Darwinian competition, cooperation, and evolution played out in real time, right before his eyes. What he discovered was that under certain conditions, the network encouraged a strong tendency to cooperate. That finding, if applicable to the real world, suggests that cooperation could indeed be a survival strategy that has been bred into our genes.

If my brother will forgive me the crude example, our altruistic willingness to help Sunny, Gary, and Pete ended up enhancing Alan's prospects for reproduction. We didn't make that calculation consciously, but the tendency to be nice guys had perhaps been bred into us over generations.

Oh, and reinforced by Mom just to make sure.

In nature, however, altruism is found in very few species. That has raised a question: If helping others were really a successful strategy in nature, not just in simulated computer networks, why isn't it more widespread?

Again, Axelrod may provide a clue. In his simulations, he found that three conditions had to exist for his agents to evolve an inclination to cooperate. If any of the three conditions was not met, cooperation would become a losing strategy, and the altruistic tendency would be bred out of the population.

First, the agents had to encounter one another repeatedly. That makes sense. If you're only going to see a person once, there's a strong temptation to try to cheat him, because you know that the other person will never be in a position to take revenge. That explains why even now, years after it has become a joke, you continue to get those Nigerian bank-scam e-mails. The con artist risks nothing in sending the offers out, and great reward if just one or two happen to pay off.

Second, the computer agents had to be able to recognize one another. And third, they had to be able to remember their previous encounters. In terms of the game, Agent 67 would not only need to recognize that its partner this time is Agent 42. It would also have to remember that Agent 42 had cooperated the last three times they interacted, so it probably has a moral code that would drive it to cooperate this time as well.

The three conditions necessary to evolve toward cooperation, then, are repetition, recognition, and remembering. In a social setting in which the three Rs exist, agents will want to be known as someone who plays well with others, so that others will in turn play well with them. Those agents who do not cooperate, who develop a reputation as cheaters . . . well, over time nobody will do business with them, and they'll fade from the scene.

Overall, the implication of Axelrod's research is as old as the Bible: "Do unto others as you would have them do unto you."

In later experiments, Axelrod discovered that cooperation became even more robust if he established "neighborhoods" where agents were able to build long histories of each other's behavior. But in networks where the agents communicated at random and had little or no history with each other, cooperation broke down and rampant cheating became the norm.

Among other things, Axelrod's findings confirm the centrality of narrative in the human experience. Remember, cooperation is a viable strategy only when we interact repeatedly with the same people, when we remember how they treated us, and when all parties know that we are likely to encounter each other in the future. It is past, present, and future.

Narrative is how the human mind keeps track of all that, how we manage to keep our heads in the game. Without narrative, life is reduced to a series of disconnected events, and the incentive to cooperate is diminished. A world in which narrative has lost its footing, in which we deal more and more often with hundreds of nameless, faceless people somewhere out there in the ether, no longer meets Axelrod's conditions. The importance of reputation disappears, the Golden Rule becomes tarnished, and defection—each of us out for himself—rather than cooperation becomes the dominant strategy.

That would seem to bode ill for cooperation in a network culture. But Axelrod's work also has its optimistic implications. If there truly is a competitive advantage to cooperation, then it seems likely that over the generations we humans may have evolved a biological drive, even a need, to cooperate.

I do know that there's a real pleasure in working together with these guys on this trip, a pleasure that feels primal and instinctive. Yes, it makes practical sense to help one another, but that doesn't explain the comfort I take in their presence and companionship.

I look up to see Richard pointing ahead to the right bank. Two cars are parked along the road, no doubt driven there by fishermen who came as far as they could by car and then headed upstream on foot or on trail bikes. We've reached Locked Gate, the beginning of public access. There's usually a large Dumpster here so groups floating downstream can pull over and unload accumulated garbage.

Alan, at the oars of our raft, starts pulling hard against the current, to get us to shore. Behind us I can see Marv and Stew doing the same.

As soon as we beach, I struggle up the steep bank with a black plastic bag in each hand, each bag swollen with trash and dripping some unknown liquid. Richard follows with the third. We dump the bags in the bin, and as we come back down the bank, we pass Marv and Stewart on their way up, also burdened with trash.

When we get back to the boat, we crack open the first cold beers of the day and sit, enjoying the warm sun, until Marv and Stew come back from the Dumpster. When we push off again a few minutes later, Richard has taken the oars. He'll be guiding us through the next major rapid, Wapinitia.

As we make our way downstream under a blue sky and increasing heat, we see more and more cars and trucks parked along the bank. The morning clouds are gone, and it's another hot day. At several points, families and groups of teenagers have set up camp right on the river. They wave as we float past, and we wave back. In one camp, a radio plays loudly, the sound carrying for hundreds of yards across the open water. I wince, but it's a harbinger of what's to come.

About twenty minutes later, we swing around a bend and there they are, stretched out in front of us. Probably thirty boats, some in single file, some clumped together, with still more preparing to launch from a large parking lot on the right bank. Most of them have six to eight people on board, each equipped with a paddle.

An ancient blue school bus, crammed with people and pulling a trailer packed high with still more rafts, has just pulled into the lot, trailing dust behind it.

The sight forces a mental adjustment. A shifting of gears, to use the industrial metaphor, or a slight reprogramming, if you prefer the electronic version. The river is no longer a wilderness setting. From here on down, it will be like a visit to a water park, with the same cast of characters attracted to it, doing roughly the same thing.

But add excessive alcohol, and subtract adult supervision.

The crowds also mean that we'll be coming up on Wapinitia fairly soon. We check to make sure that everything's strapped down tight. As I pull on my life jacket, Alan moves to the bow of the raft. He's going to go bronco riding.

He positions himself with legs dangling off the front, and holds on to the bow rope between his legs with his right hand. Then he throws his left arm up and behind him. "Yeeeee-haww!" he shouts, warming up for the ride ahead.

As the head of Wapinitia comes into view, we can see half a dozen rafts in various sections of the rapids. Richard pulls back on the oars, delaying our entry to create some space between us and the boats ahead. One of the quickest ways to get into trouble on a rapids is to get caught up with another craft, leaving yourself no room to maneuver.

Now we're set. Richard points us right down the middle of the V-slick, then moves quickly over to the right to avoid the rocks. So far so good. Then the raft hits a series of high-standing waves, and the bow rises up toward the sky, then dips down into a deep trough, then back up the next wave.

It's like a roller coaster—from crest to trough the wave is probably eight feet—and as the bow hits the crest of the second wave, I can see about six inches of sunlight appear between Alan's butt and the bow of the raft.

"Yeeee-haw!" he yells, then comes smashing down onto the raft again, losing his balance and almost pitching headfirst into the water. We climb up the next wave, and once again he catches some good air. As they say in the rodeo, he's drawn a good bronc. Up, down, up down, and then we're through the worst of it.

Alan wipes the spray from his face with his free hand, then points downstream.

"Look there," he says.

At the bottom of the rapids, a couple of hundred yards downstream, the main current passes between two large rock formations. All boats traveling this section have to pass through that bottleneck. And perched on the rocks on either side of the channel are about a dozen guys, armed with water guns, hooting and hollering. They've tied their boats to the rocks behind them and have set up a gauntlet.

We watch as the boat ahead of us slides through and is met by a barrage of water from both sides. After it finally clears the strait, its passengers completely waterlogged, their assailants rise to cheer in triumph.

"They think they're goddamned pirates or something," Alan says, swinging his legs back inside the raft.

"Well, we've got no choice. We've gotta go right through them," Richard says. "Get ready. We're gonna get smashed."

"Those guys are smashed already. They look like they've been drinking all day."

"Hey, Alan," I say. "Let's pick out one guy. Pick out the biggest son of a bitch in the bunch, and we'll nail him. We're gonna get soaked anyway, we might as well leave a mark."

"Okay," Alan says, surveying our possible targets. "How about the one standing up, the guy hooting and hollering and pointing at us right now?"

"The pasty face with the Yankee hat? Hey, he even looks like George Steinbrenner. Perfect."

I dip the end of a water gun into the river and then draw it back, filling it with water, then repeat it with our second gun. Alan, up at the front, dips his bucket deep into the water and then struggles with the weight of it as he brings it back into the boat.

The current draws us closer. The pirates stand and taunt us. At least we have the breeze behind us. Shooting upwind, their water guns can't quite reach us yet.

"Don't fire until you see the whites of their eyes," says Richard, making his final adjustments at the oars to align us with the channel.

"Let me fire first, bro, then you," I tell Alan, who has crouched as low as he can in the front of the boat, out of the line of fire. The bucket sits between his knees, brimming with water. He nods and smiles.

I tighten the strap holding my wraparound sunglasses in place, then stand up. I want to draw as much of their fire as I can before unloading my own weapon, and in a few seconds my wish comes true. I get blasted by water guns, from both sides. It's hard to see through the spray, hard even to stand, and I'm vaguely aware of loud hooting and hollering around me.

My sunglasses, though, act like a diver's mask, allowing me to keep my eyes open. As soon as I sense a lull in the barrage, I raise my head, pick out Steinbrenner there on the left, and let him have it, right in the face, full force.

I catch him as he's leaning down, reloading his gun, and he isn't prepared. He closes his eyes and throws his hands up to protect himself, and the stream of water knocks his Yankee hat off his head into the river behind him. As soon as I exhaust my ammunition, Alan stands, spots him, and really lets him have it, a full bucketload, right in the side of his face, from about five feet away.

Then things start to happen in slow motion: Steinbrenner, his hat gone, starts to teeter backward on the narrow rock. He loses his balance, and as he opens his mouth to take a gasp of air I hit him with the contents of the second gun, again right in the face.

He tumbles off the rock and into the water behind him, reaching out for something to break his fall but finding only air.

"Yes!" yells Richard, still at the oars, trying to peer through the deluge of water still coming at us from both sides. "Nailed him!"

Alan is trying to reload his bucket, and I'm leaning over the side, refilling my water gun, but now we're paying the price. There's so much water flying at us from both directions that it's like we're going through a car wash. By the time we've managed to reload, it's too late. We've floated downstream, out of range.

Alan and I high-five, grinning, then look back. Marv and Stewie are about to run the gauntlet themselves. Stewie's standing at the bow, armed with a water gun, laughing in glee.

"Hey look!" Richard points off to our left. Steinbrenner is floating in the current about thirty feet away from us. He isn't wearing a life jacket—pirates are apparently too cool for that—and he's struggling. In fact, he's flailing in the water, trying to fight against the current and yelling for help from his buddies, none of whom has even noticed that he's gone. They're all too busy trying to nail Marv and Stew.

Damn.

Richard glances downstream, assessing our position, then swings the bow to the left and starts pushing us toward the guy as fast as he can.

"Over here!" Alan yells, trying to get Steinbrenner's attention. "Over here!"

"Alan! The bow rope! Toss him the bow rope!"

Alan grabs the yellow nylon rope. It's only about twenty feet long—we're not close enough yet. Richard pushes hard on the oars, trying to cut across the swift flow of water washing us downstream.

I start peeling off my life jacket. Alan is yelling, but he still can't get the guy's attention. He doesn't know we're over here, and, oh my God, his head just went under water.

Man, this is looking bad.

There he is, back up, but struggling.

I get the jacket off and reach back like a discus thrower, trying to gauge the distance. Got to land it a little upstream of him, so he'll see it and can let it float to him.

A couple of false throws, just to get the distance right. Then I fling it as far as I can.

Not perfect, but good enough.

Steinbrenner sees the life jacket splash in front of him, then looks over, startled, trying to see where it came from. His panicked expression doesn't change, but he manages to swim a stroke or two upstream, just enough to bring the jacket within reach. Then he hugs it to him like a mother clinging to a lost baby.

Alan, still in the bow, tosses the rope out toward him but it comes up short. Richard is still pushing us over that way with the oars, but we've got to get to him soon. Rocks loom on the left. If he hits those he's in trouble, and so are we.

I look upstream. Marv and Stewie have run the gauntlet and are looking our way. Everybody on the rocks is staring downstream at us as well. Then a mad scramble begins among the pirates as they head to their boats, leaving water guns and beer cans strewn all over the rocks.

Alan pulls the rope back into the boat, coiling it into his hand again. He makes another throw, and this time the rope slaps across the life jacket. Steinbrenner grabs it.

"Hold on!" Richard says, and he starts pulling hard on the oars the other way, working desperately to get us back into the main channel, away from the rocks. Alan pulls the rope in, hand over hand. Steinbrenner clings to the life jacket with one hand, to the rope with the other. As he comes our way his feet float up behind him and he starts skimming over the surface, almost like he's water-skiing. When he reaches the side of the raft I grab him under the left arm, Alan grabs the other arm, and in one motion we hoist him on board and onto the floor of the raft.

"Sit down! Sit down! I can't see!" Richard yells, and Alan and I collapse into our seats.

Richard pulls hard once, twice, and then we hit the rock bow first.

The contact spins us around, and we pass safely through the last rapid tail first, then out into calmer water.

"He all right?" Richard says, nodding toward our passenger. The guy's lying on the floor of the raft, not moving much.

"You okay?" Alan asks, reaching down to touch his shoulder.

"Yeah. Just give me a minute," the guy says, trying to catch his breath. A few moments later he starts to sit up. "Shit, you guys nailed me."

"I think he's fine," Alan reports to Richard, chuckling a little bit. "But what do we do with prisoners of war?"

"Torture 'em?" I suggest.

The guy starts to laugh, then chokes again, coughing his guts out.

"Thanks," he finally says, once he recovers his breath. By now, Richard has pulled us over to the right bank. Upstream I can see Marv and Stewie coming up fast behind us, with a flotilla of three or four boats trailing them, coming to reclaim their lost mate.

"Hey, you guys didn't happen to get my hat, did you? I think you knocked it off up there."

"That Yankees cap? Sorry," Alan says. "There's a limit to our charity."

I see the guy's eyes travel from Alan's face to the battered Red Sox cap on top of his head, then to mine.

"Sox fans? I got rescued by Sox fans?"

"You did. But not your damn hat."

"Shit. We're kicking your ass again this year, you know."

Alan looks up at me and winces.

"I think we caught some type of bottom-feeding fish here, brother. Think we ought to throw him back?"

But we don't, of course. A few minutes later Marv and Stew pull up alongside us, with the pirate flotilla close behind. We surrender our prisoner to them, and Richard and I exchange places. He's gotten us through Wapinitia; now it's my turn to take us through Boxcar, a class 4 rapid just a few hundred yards ahead. It can do you some serious harm if you're not careful.

By pulling over here, though, we've lost our place in the line of boats moving through this section. We've got to wait a few minutes, like a car waiting to merge onto the interstate, until the heavier traffic passes.

I once read a first-person account of the first expedition to boat through this part of the Deschutes, published in a Portland newspaper back in the 1920s or 1930s. At the end of the piece, the author concluded that no other crew was likely ever to repeat his group's feat unless, as he put it, some future thrill seekers happened to give it a try.

I wonder what he would think of all this. Everywhere you look—rafts full of adrenaline junkies. Me included. I've handled Boxcar more than a dozen times with no problem, but the anxiety I feel as I hear the rumble of crashing water and the high-pitched screams of excitement from other boaters as they head into the chute . . . it's something you never encounter in day-to-day life. That excitement is undoubtedly part of the reason we come out here.

I never really appreciated the impact of adrenaline on the brain, at least not in scientific terms, until a couple of years ago, when I went over to Emory University to write about its new fMRI machine, for functional magnetic resonance imaging. Rather than study the anatomical structures of the human brain, as a regular MRI would, the fMRI reveals how the various parts of the brain actually function.

Using a powerful magnetic field, the fMRI tracks tiny flows of blood to various parts of the brain. Where blood flow increases, brain activity has increased as well. Once the data are processed through a computer graphics program, the fMRI produces an accurate rendering of which parts of the brain are used to complete a given mental task, or which parts are excited by a given stimulus.

"Seeing this, you really begin to appreciate the brain's complexity, how it works together as a network," Dr. Stephan Hamann told me, gesturing to a computer-generated image of a brain at work. "What you see is an awful lot going on in the brain at once, not just in one or two areas but all over."

Using the fMRI and other tools, scientists have mapped the regions and structures of the brain, and for the most part know their functions. The challenge now is to document how those various parts cooperate to produce human consciousness.

Hamann and other researchers are using imaging technology to explore the brains of violent criminals, and to watch the physical changes produced in the brain by drugs such as Ritalin. Some scientists claim they can watch a person's brain as he studies photographs and determine whether he harbors racist sentiments. Others say they can look into the mind of a murder suspect and determine whether he has memories—conscious or unconscious—of the crime. By determining what part of the brain is being used, scientists can also tell whether a person acquired a particular language as a child or as an adult, or whether she's seeing the face of someone of her own or a different race.

"We've even joked about finding the part of the brain that wants to understand how the brain works," Hamann told me.

Later, after we talked a few more minutes, Hamann asked me to lie down on a gurney. After fixing my head into place with an inflatable collar, he and his assistant rolled me into the machine and ran through abbreviated versions of several research projects. In one experiment, Hamann showed me a series of photographs, some pleasant, some negative. He asked me to concentrate for a few seconds on each image as the fMRI scanned my brain activity.

A few days later, I went back to the lab to see the results. The scan taken as I viewed positive images showed a relatively quiet brain, with patches of activity. But when I was shown negative images—mainly scenes of violence and death—the picture was very different.

Confronted with ugly images, my hippocampus and amygdala, deep in the center of my brain, showed intense activity. Those areas are part of the limbic system, the brain's more primitive, emotional side, the part that gets off on the thrill of floating through white water. I dislike violence in movies as a matter of principle. But my brain is no respecter of my principles—as the fMRI showed, it goes all atwitter when confronted with violence.

In fact, gratuitous violence isn't gratuitous at all to the amygdala and the hippocampus. They live for it. When Hollywood producers pump up the body count in a movie, my amygdala and hippocampus are their target audience.

Since my visit, researchers at Emory have put the fMRI to another use, monitoring what happens to the human brain in a social interaction.

Researchers asked their test subjects—all women, in this instance—to play the same basic game that Axelrod had used in his computer tournaments. The human subjects were promised monetary rewards depending on how many points they accumulated in the game.

Throughout each game, the brain of one player was monitored with the fMRI. And it quickly became apparent that, as in the Axelrod work, the win-win strategy of mutual cooperation was both popular and profitable among the human subjects.

In fact, during periods of mutual cooperation, researchers found a high degree of activity in two so-called pleasure centers of the brain, and the players themselves reported warm, pleasant feelings. In sessions where the women knew that their playing partner was actually a computer, not a human being, they still tended to cooperate, but in those circumstances their pleasure centers were significantly less stimulated.

Those findings are rich in implications, particularly when viewed in light of Axelrod's work. Axelrod demonstrated how evolution might have hard-wired us to cooperate and make sacrifices for each other, at least theoretically. The work at Emory and elsewhere suggests that such hard-wiring may indeed have occurred, since cooperation does stimulate the primitive pleasure centers deep within the brain.

Simplicity also turns out to be important, though. In Kauffman's research at the Santa Fe Institute, he has found that emergent stability and order depend heavily on how "connected" each node is to its peers. When each node is connected to two other nodes, the order that Kauffman celebrates emerges naturally. When each node is connected to three other nodes, the system becomes more chaotic, less orderly. When each node is connected to four or more nodes, order disappears altogether and chaos reigns. There are too many messages coming in, and you get what Kauffman calls a "complexity catastrophe."

"Sparsely connected networks exhibit internal order," Kauffman concludes. "Densely connected ones veer into chaos."

Of course, human beings are far more complex than the simple nodes that Kauffman simulated on his computer. But the concept of a complexity catastrophe is intriguing because it suggests that each type of network has a maximum number of connections that it can tolerate before chaos ensues.

The procession of boats has eased a bit now, leaving an opening of a few hundred yards. Marv and Stewie go first, and we wait for them to clear. Then Alan, on the bank, gets ready to shove us off. I'm at the oars, ready to pull us into the current.

"Here we go," Alan says, and as the raft scrapes free of the riverbed, he jumps aboard. I work a spin move—back on the left oar, forward on the right one—and point the bow of the boat downstream, toward Boxcar.

The rapids are upon us quickly. Okay, here we go, here we go. . . . The current grabs us, and it's trying to shove the raft directly into the steep rock wall on the left.

I pull back on the oars, then pull back again, trying to keep the front of the raft in proper position, five to ten feet from the canyon wall.

We're moving swiftly through here, and the roar of the falls up ahead gets louder.

The handling of a raft moving through white water is hard to describe. Think of taking a car on a controlled, braking skid through an obstacle course on an ice rink, and you have some idea of what it's like with the oars in your hands. You're in control only in the most general of terms, trying to manage the physics of your situation as best you can.

We're coming to the end of the chute now. In another ten yards the river swings hard to the right. Position is crucial. Too far left or right, and the raft will flip.

So . . . swing right, not too far, not too far, just touch the right edge of that big boulder, then let the current wash us down. . . . We're clear.

"Good job!" Alan says, and I nod.

Marv and Stewart are holding in a backwater, waiting for us about a hundred yards ahead, along the right bank. Farther downstream, the water fights have begun again. Spraying arcs connect raft to raft, like rainbows; others move in close for some hand-to-hand combat with buckets. The pirate crew seems to be right in the middle of the chaos.

We pull up alongside Marv and Stewart. Richard grabs a rope on their raft and pulls the boats together in the current.

"What's up? Why you waiting here?" Alan asks.

Marv gives us a funny, almost apologetic look.

"Well . . . how bad do you guys want to go all the way down to Sandy Beach?"

Oh. My heart sinks a bit. That's what this is about.

"You thinking of pulling out early, at Maupin?" Alan asks.

"What's the matter, Marv?" Richard jumps in. "Sun getting to you, you wimp?"

"Nah, it's not the heat," Marv says. "It's the humanity. If we stay on the river it'll just be another five or six miles of that." He gestures with his head downstream, toward the armada of boats.

I look behind us. More boats are popping through Boxcar as we speak, heading our way. The Bureau of Land Management has proposed a permit system to limit use of this section, and it's hard to think of a more convincing argument than this scene.

"Plus, I've got to catch a red-eye back to Nashville at nine tonight," Stewart says. "If we pull out early, I'll get back to Portland in time to clean up before I head to the airport."

"That might be a good idea," Richard says, a little smirk in his voice. "After six days without a shower, you could kill somebody just by sitting next to him."

Everybody falls silent, deciding what to do. This was unexpected. Marv knows that he's asking a lot, and he's not going to push it. I was thinking I had a few more hours out here, and it's tough to have it snatched away. Once we're gone, we're gone for a year.

But I can also see the wisdom of what they're proposing. We've already done the rapids downstream from here so many times that they've lost some of their appeal. And from here on, it's going to be a carnival anyway. The best part of the trip, the reason we come here each year, is already over. This is just the dregs of the bottle. If we finish these last few gulps of the bottle, it'll be out of a sense of duty more than anything.

"Hey, we still have time to drive down to Sherar's Falls?" Alan asks. "I told Sunny I would get a picture of it for her. For her dad, actually."

"Yeah, sure, no problem," says Marv.

"We'll have to call the raft company when we get to Maupin, tell Johnny to deliver the Yukon to us there instead of Sandy Beach," Richard says.

So. We all look at each other. It appears to have been decided. Maupin it is.

We separate the two rafts, and I row back into the current and let us drift. It's just one long straightaway between here and Maupin, about two miles of river, and I'm not in any hurry now. None of us is. Boatloads of enthusiastic paddlers, exhilarated after Boxcar and eager to get past Maupin to the rest of the white water down below, are passing us right and left.

But we're just floating, taking in the air and the sky and the feel of the river beneath us.

Marv, still just a few feet away, points behind us. I turn, and see two boatloads of day-trippers coming up fast, teenagers, all of them paddling hard in rhythm, moving quickly with the wind and current at their backs. They have malice in their young hearts, though; as they draw closer, about fifty feet away, those up front drop their paddles and reach down to pick up water guns.

None of us moves. We just stare coldly at them, smiling inside, knowing that if they start something our own weapons are hidden within easy reach. Over the water I hear words spoken on their rafts. Some kind of disagreement is taking place. Then, slowly, the would-be gunners drop their weapons and again pick up their paddles. We've stared them down.

They move on, waving sheepishly as they pass us. We wave grimly in return. As soon as they're beyond us, focused now on catching up to the next armada of rafts, I grab the oars and start rowing downstream, trying quietly to keep pace. Marv takes my cue and does the same. Alan, Richard, and Stew realize what we're up to and load their water guns.

As we draw within range, still undetected, our three gunners send arcs of water high up in the air, letting the wind carry it right onto the two boatloads ahead of us.

The kids look around, startled to find sheets of water falling on them out of a clear blue desert sky. When they turn to see us, the expressions of surprise, recognition, and outrage are enough to set all of us laughing in delight.

Our gunners reload and send another barrage of water their way, again hitting the target. The kids scramble, trying desperately to come back upstream against the current to get us, but it's too late. Marv and I simply pull back on the oars, staying well out of their range, chuckling all the time. For these last few minutes we are little boys at play, innocent and wicked.

Finally their paddlers tire under the strain, abandoning their effort to come back upstream to get us.

Up ahead, I can see the black steel Maupin bridge, looming like a finish line. Just beyond it is the city park, where we'll be pulling out. Along the left rim of the canyon, new buildings rise up out of the desert, homes of fresh lumber being built right on the cliff, looking down into the river. The outskirts of Maupin have moved probably half a mile upstream in the years we've been making the trip.

Then we pass beneath the bridge. I start pulling hard to the right, toward the city park crammed with pickup trucks and camping trailers, each with its own satellite dish on the roof.

epilogue

Peering into the cracked, darkened mirror in the county park rest room, I see a homeless person peering back. After a week in the harsh desert sun, my eyes are rimmed in red, and tufts of hair sprout from my face. But for the first time in a week, my hair is combed. It may be dirty, stringy, and greasy, but it's combed.

My clothes are clean and presentable too, right down to fresh underwear. And the weight of the wallet riding in my back pocket for the first time in a week feels both odd and oddly familiar.

It has taken us less than an hour to unload the rafts, toss the gear in the trailer, and change into "civilian" clothes, ready for the ride home. Years ago it would have taken longer, but by now we work together with exquisite military precision.

Well, more or less.

We have one more stop before we head home, though. The five of us climb into the Yukon and head north along the river, toward Sherar's Falls, so Alan can take his promised pictures for Sunny. After a week spent outdoors, surrounded by nothing but desert breezes, it feels strange to shut ourselves into a container, enclosed by metal, glass, chrome, and leather, with the air conditioner blasting. The smooth asphalt beneath us feels foreign as well, quite unlike the constant rocking of the raft.

The clock on the dashboard reads 3:15 P.M.

I'm sitting in the backseat this time, behind Richard at the steering wheel, looking out the window into the canyon about a hundred feet below us. A long line of brightly colored boats is picking its way through the shoals and rocks. The rafts look so small from up here, the rapids even smaller.

The falls are only six miles away, so this little side trip won't take long. We pass a steady stream of traffic coming from the other direction, ferrying sunburned rafters back into town.

Up ahead, the shoulder of the road is crowded with cars. We've reached Oak Springs, the biggest rapid on this lower section. Sightseers line the banks here to watch the rafters and kayakers come through, like NASCAR crowds at the first turn waiting for spectacular crashes. On a crowded day like today, they'll probably see a few.

At forty miles per hour, we cover a lot of river quickly. In another couple of minutes we reach Sandy Beach, the takeout point just above Sherar's Falls. No boats are allowed to pass below this point; because of the falls ahead, this is the end of the rafting through this section.

Probably two hundred people are milling around the large gravel parking lot as we drive by. Piles of wet gear drip under the brutal sun, and a long line of people stands at the rest rooms. Cars, trucks, buses, and trailers come and go constantly, kicking up dust that swirls away in the hot wind.

"Good thing we got out of the river at Maupin," Richard says softly. The rest of us sit in mute agreement, staring out the windows. Dealing with that mob scene would have done serious damage to our river-induced serenity.

Finally, up ahead, spray seems to be rising from the middle of the desert: Sherar's Falls. We clear a ridge and it comes clearly into view.

It's a stunning sight. Here the entire volume of the river is funneled through a narrow slot in the hard volcanic basalt, falling about twenty feet in the process. This is a class 6 rapid, impassable by most types of boats. Even the stubborn salmon and steelhead have a hard time negotiating this obstacle, so a fish ladder has been installed along the opposite bank, allowing them easier passage to spawning areas and a hatchery upstream.

Richard brings the Yukon to a crunching halt in the gravel, and we all climb out.

The dull roar of the falls hits us as soon as the car doors open. I stand there, taking in the view, while Richard, Alan, and Stewart start ambling down toward the river. No one else is around. This time of year, the place is a little out of the way for sightseers, and most of the rafters have other priorities.

Marv, standing by the side of the road, pulls out a cell phone to call home, to let everyone know that we've come off the river and have survived another year. I'm not sure he can get a call through from out here, but apparently he does. He starts talking loudly, telling someone a story. I hear the word "Whitehorse" as he glances in my direction and smiles.

Great.

This is our good-bye to the river for the year, and there's one more thing I have to do before we leave. I look around, finally spotting what I need up a little hill on the other side of the road, overlooking the falls.

I struggle up the dusty hillside, the deep bruise on my thigh still hurting when I climb. Once at the top, I pull out my pocketknife and saw off several sprigs of sagebrush to pack away in my baggage and take home to Atlanta. We use the sage in cooking—it's great with butter on boiled potatoes—and on occasion I'll even crumble it between my fingers and let the aroma fill my nostrils and my brain. It never fails to bring me back here.

Wonder what that would look like on an fMRI brain scan.

I fold the knife and slip it into my pocket, then turn to look back at the river, clutching the sage in my hand like a bouquet of flowers I'm bringing to a girlfriend.

Down below, Marv is still on the cell phone. Alan, Stew, and Richard have made their way down to the falls, and are taking pictures of each other with Sunny's camera, posing with the falls as a backdrop. The angle of the afternoon sun creates a rainbow tinge through the mist.

I start thinking about what might have happened in the real world this week. Before we left, President Bush had been making noises about going to war with Iraq, and the stock market—who can predict what that might have done? It was falling like a rock the week we left.

Out on the river, the reality of being disconnected from all that seemed perfectly normal. But already I can feel myself changing. I can't wait to get my hands on a newspaper, to catch up on what I missed.

Probably not much. August is the slowest news time of the year. Stories that ordinarily might not even make the paper can become page-one sensations because there's not much competition for people's attention. The news business doesn't stop just because the news does.

But the river does change your perspective. You realize that the world goes on without you, and that you can go on without the world. You come to appreciate the honesty and clarity of seeing things, hearing things, feeling and experiencing things firsthand.

I promise myself to try to nurture that thought, to remember what this feels like in the weeks and months to come.

It won't be easy though. In the world to which we return, we will be surrounded by simulation and stimulation, and simulated stimulation. The effect can be soul-numbing.

It's numbing in another way as well. Because it is so draining to constantly try to cull the useful from the useless out of the flood of data sent our way, I'm afraid too many people no longer even try. For those of us who do pay attention, change occurs so quickly that any insight or understanding we might pluck from the data stream has a half-life measured in days if not hours before it is contradicted by something else. It's just damn hard trying to comprehend all we see.

The situation reminds me of those people who, after many years of blindness, are suddenly given the gift of vision. They can perceive light and color and movement—their optic nerve now delivers all the information to their brain that a sighted person sees. But they are lost because they have never learned how to make sense of all that data.

They have no patterns in their brains to match against the patterns of what they see. They cannot know that a hat looks like a hat, or a bird looks like a bird, or that brown is brown. They cannot recognize shapes or structures. They "see" it all, yet they can't connect the dots.

And so it is for us. Data we've got. Megabytes, gigabytes, terabytes of data, standing waves of data, coming at us constantly, but we have no capacity to put it into context. "With instant information, there's no longer any time for history," as French philosopher Jean Baudrillard puts it. ". . . In a sense, it doesn't have time to take place."

That disorientation is part of the price we pay for plugging into the network, the web that connects each of us to everybody, and everybody to each of us. As long as we are linked to the network, our attention is no longer our own, to be parceled out as we see fit. We have placed it in the control of others.

To preserve this peace of mind, I will try to remember to unplug from time to time. Ignorance is not an option, but occasional clarity is important as well. I remember something I learned a long time ago from my father, when I was a kid and he was teaching me to shoot a rifle.

If you've ever gone shooting, you know that if you stare too hard down the gunsight, your eyes begin to water and you can't see clearly. The target becomes blurry and indistinct, and staring harder only makes things worse.

"Look away from the target; find something green and far away to look at," Dad would tell me. "It'll ease the strain and let you focus."

He was right; it does.

Other challenges, unfortunately, are more complicated, beyond the power of Dad's advice, beyond the power of any one individual to affect.

My premise from the beginning has been that Western culture, and by extension the entire world, is in the midst of a historic technology-driven transformation. If that's correct, if we are indeed in the midst of a great transition to a network culture, we are also experiencing what William Ogburn in 1922 aptly called a "culture lag."

Ogburn understood that at certain points in history, technology can change at such a rapid pace that it leaves the rest of society in its wake. Institutions, laws, ideologies, and even leaders that had served a public need in the previous world are rendered archaic in the new one, creating a vacuum of sorts. The result is a society stripped of its coping mechanisms and struggling to regain its footing.

The most obvious example is the Islamic world, struggling today with a culture lag measured not in years or decades but centuries, its institutions spectacularly ill-suited to handle the demands of the modern world.

In Western history, the most prominent example is the Industrial Revolution, when the swift conversion from a rural, almost feudal culture to the machine age rendered the existing communal arrangements all but useless. The resulting culture lag was profound, and through a painful, lengthy, and often violent process of adaptation, new institutions were created, and existing institutions were forced to assume new forms and new responsibilities.

Government, for example, had to intervene much more forcefully in economic affairs to protect workers and the environment. Employees unable to find security on their own united to form labor unions to give themselves more control over their fate. Even communism can be seen as an effort to obliterate the culture lag in one rather audacious leap, and in the process redress the imbalances of power and wealth that had been created.

Today we face a dislocation that is equally profound. But for the moment, I think, we're still too transfixed by the marvels of the change occurring all around us to start addressing the lag. The idea that technology can and must be guided to some degree, that we can try to assert control over this transformation just as we control everything else around us, is apparently still too much for us to accept.

But perhaps the best way to describe the challenges of the twenty-first century is in terms of network dynamics. Indeed, if you tried to view all of human history through that particular lens, it would look something like this:

From the beginning of time, we have turned to the collective to impose order on the chaos around us, to protect us from the cruel randomness of nature, and from the cruelty of each other. In tribe, clan, king, and nation we found a reassuring source of control and security. It's what we are trained by evolution to seek and want.

But we also paid a price for that. In those times and places when the collective has been too powerful, it has stifled human freedom and repressed change, making the system static and freezing us in place, allowing little or no innovation. That has in fact been the human condition for most of our species' history, and even today it remains the case for much of mankind.

But over the last five hundred years, beginning with the invention of the transoceanic sailing ship and the printing press, that began to change, at least in the West. As communication improved and the network culture began to rise and take a crude early form, the grip of the collective slowly began to weaken, allowing the individual— the agent of chaos—to emerge as a dominant influence on history.

The church lost power. Kings were executed. Declarations of independence were issued. Bills of rights were written.

In time the railroad, the telegraph, the automobile, broke the collective down still further. Change accelerated, personal freedom accelerated, and as they did, even more forms of communication emerged, further hastening the decline of the collective. Communication continued to replace community.

Today, with cell phones and the Internet connecting all to all, we have undergone a transition from a static system in which nothing much changed for centuries at a time to a dynamic system that is rich in invention and change and excitement. We are perched on that precipice between order and chaos, the social equivalent of biology's ecotone, the rich and diverse transition zone between one thing and another, the edge between meadow and forest, forest and desert, desert and river.

But even there, at the glorious edge between chaos and order, the collective remains an essential resource. If a network culture self-organizes, it will do so just as it did in the Industrial Revolution, by creating new forms of the collective and forcing new roles upon old institutions.

And in the end, there is still the Question:

There's no doubt that artistically, intellectually, and economically the edge between order and chaos is where we are most productive.

But I am not sure that the degree of chaos that makes us most productive, and the degree of chaos that we as humans are willing to tolerate over the long term, are one and the same. In fact, I see no reason to believe it could be. Just as we were designed by evolution to crave as many sweets as possible, even if it now makes us obese, just as we were designed to take in as much information as possible, even if it now makes us a little crazy, we were also designed by evolution to seek security.

It may well be that the aeons in which our ancestors fought so hard against the randomness of nature have genetically biased us toward a culture that approaches but ultimately pulls back from the edge of swirling chaos. Or, if we decide we want the benefits that life on the edge may bring, we may have no choice but to compensate by finding other means, through the collective, of making the randomness of that approach more tolerable.

A networked economy, for example, will probably cycle from boom to bust and back to boom again much more quickly, for reasons less and less apparent to us, because information will be moving at ever greater velocity through the system. Given that reality, I marvel at the global trend toward dismantling the social safety net. It may be consistent with the ideology driving change today, but it seems to me an ideology ill-suited to the new world we are building. Our inability to understand that is evidence of the culture lag afflicting us.

In other ways, you can already see halting changes under way that attempt to restore some degree of stability to this fractious world. The growing appeal of religious fundamentalism and mysticism in cultures around the globe is a natural reaction to the chaos that people feel around them, and to the sense that they have lost control.

Here in the United States, the withdrawal of so many into "planned communities," gated retreats that tolerate only a very narrow range of behaviors, possibilities, and socioeconomic classes, may be another symptom. That sense of something unfulfilled may also explain the growth of suburban megachurches, drawing massive congregations from those eager to belong to something that offers identity and meaning.

The rising militarism of the American people may also be a

reaction to the insecurity that pervades modern life. By rights, we ought to feel more secure than any people who have ever lived on this planet. We have friendly Canada to the north and Mexico to the south, with major oceans on either side. We spend more on our military than all the rest of the world combined.

Yet still we are frightened. Why? September 11 does not fully explain it, because our insecurity clearly predated those events. I have a feeling that even if we spent twice as much on defense, or three times as much, that feeling of fear and insecurity would not diminish. It comes from a source that military power cannot assault.

"None of our societies knows how to manage its mourning for the real, for power, for the social itself," says Baudrillard. "What society seeks through production and overproduction is the restoration of the real, which escapes it."

The modern predicament reminds me of those Chinese finger traps, the paper toys that grip you tighter the more you struggle to escape. The harder we fight for a sense of personal security and identity, insinuating new technologies into every aspect of our lives to make ourselves more productive and competitive, the less secure we actually feel.

And the less secure we feel, the harder we chase what we can never catch. If we allow them, collective institutions can act as shock absorbers, slowing things down to a humanly comprehensible pace. They can give us a sense of conscious control over our fates. They can ensure that network culture does not sacrifice human needs in pursuit of efficiency.

Those needs, after all, will not allow themselves to go unmet. The tragic history of the twentieth century, in which an unaddressed culture lag drove otherwise civilized people to seek shelter in evil men and evil ideologies, offers a warning to those who would risk such a step in the twenty-first, when the potential tools of control and repression are so much more potent.

Either way, this is not, finally, a problem of technology. A technology that is driven by a different understanding, by different visions of human capacity and goals, would produce a different outcome for us.

Over by the falls, I see Alan, Richard, and Stewart slowly, reluctantly, turn their backs on the river and start making their way toward the Yukon, talking quietly. Marv, seeing them approach, cuts short his conversation, punches a button with his thumb, and starts to slide the cell phone into his shirt pocket.

Stewart gestures to him to keep the phone out; I can't hear what they're saying, but it looks as though Stewart wants to call home.

I watch the four of them, joking among themselves as Stewart and Marv start play-wrestling for possession of the phone. Marv holds it well over his head, out of Stewart's reach, as if he were playing with a dog. Stewart leaps once or twice for it, then finally puts a bear hug around Marv's waist and raises him easily off the ground. I can hear their laughter even over the roar of the falls.

Boose . . . I'll be seeing him again at the family Thanksgiving, just three months from now. Is it possible he'll bring Sunny? I guess a lot depends on how their September trip goes.

Marv, he's already made plans to come by Atlanta next spring, on his way to attend the Talladega 500 in Alabama. It's his personal life mission to attend all of the major sporting events, from the Masters to the World Series to the Final Four. He's trying to drag me along with him this time, to camp on the Talladega infield in an RV, along with thousands of other race fans. Boy howdy.

Stewart, my brother-in-law, lives just up the interstate in Nashville—I'll no doubt see him several times before next year's trip. Even Richard ends up traveling through Atlanta on business now and again.

But seeing these guys individually, back in the real world, is never the same as seeing them all together here on the river. In real life our paths may intersect now and again; out here, for a week at least, those paths run parallel, right down this canyon.

Out there, we operate more or less as a network, each of us an independent node communicating with other nodes. On the river it's a community, a fellowship.

And now it's about to break up. In just a few minutes, we'll all be packed into the Yukon again, this time heading west over Mount Hood, back into the traffic and bustle of Portland.

And if past trips are any guide, the five of us will sit through the return trip in dead silence, in part because we're exhausted, in part because we'll each be running through our heads the list of things we have to do upon reentry to the world.

Tonight, after a hot shower and a shave at the motel, I'll probably make some phone calls and grab as many newspapers as I can find. And when I finally crawl into the soft bed, putting my freshly laundered self between freshly laundered sheets, I'll feel like I'm staying at the Ritz.

But when I look up, I know, I'll see a white plaster ceiling, not a black bowl of stars. And when I finally close my eyes, I may think I smell, will want to smell, the scent of sage in the air-conditioned room and hear the river running somewhere in the background, but these sensations will be punctuated by the sounds of horns honking and a television booming the ESPN theme song in the room next door.

For the moment, though, the roar of the river and the heat of the dying day are still real enough.

The falls look empty now, almost abandoned. Just downstream, ramshackle Indian fishing platforms reach out over the water, much as they had extended for centuries over Celilo Falls about twenty-five miles north of here.

The tribes still have the right, under the treaty of 1855, to fish the salmon and steelhead runs that come through here to spawn. Federal law prohibits the Indians from selling what they catch. The fish can be used only for ceremonial or subsistence purposes. But each spring and fall, the Indians come here to fish anyway, using long-handled dip nets much like those of their ancestors.

Tourists come too, sitting on the banks where I'm now standing and watching as if the Indians were some living history exhibit. I wonder how many of the onlookers understand the importance of what they are seeing: human beings who have been caught in the current of rapid change, and in some ways denied control of their own fate, still fighting against daunting odds to maintain a connection to their past, and more important, to each other.

Yes, there's a sadness there, but in the stubborn, insistent heroism of their struggle, you have to believe there is cause for hope as well.

I start picking my way down the steep hillside toward the Yukon. The moment has come; it's time to go home.

about the author

Jay Bookman, a columnist and editor for *The Atlanta Journal-Constitution*, has twice been recognized as the nation's outstanding editorial writer. His columns have appeared in more than fifty newspapers around the country and in newspapers in Asia, Europe, and South America. He lives in Atlanta with his wife and two daughters.